NO BIG DEAL

A Guide to Recovery from Addictions

John Coats

First published September 2006

reprinted May 2009

Copyright © John Coats 2006

The right of John Coats to be identified
as the author of this work has been asserted
by him in accordance with the
Copyright, Designs and Patents Act, 1988

First published in Great Britain in 2006 by
The Sow's Ear Press
School House, Alby Hill, Aldborough
Norwich NR11 7PH

British Library Cataloguing in Publication Data.
A catalogue record for this book is available from the British Library.

ISBN-10: 0-9553677-0-0

ISBN-13: 978-0-9553677-0-0

The Twelve Steps are reprinted and adapted and brief excerpts from the book, *Alcoholics Anonymous* are reprinted with permission of Alcoholics Anonymous World Services, Inc. (AAWS). Permission to reprint brief excerpts from the book, *Alcoholics Anonymous* and the Twelve Steps does not mean that AAWS has reviewed or approved the contents of this publication, or that AAWS necessarily agrees with the views expressed herein.
A.A. is a program of recovery from alcoholism only - use of the Twelve Steps in connection with programs and activities which are patterned after A.A., but which address other problems, or in any other non-A.A. context, does not imply otherwise.

Printed by Barnwell Print Ltd., Aylsham, Norfolk NR11 6SU. Tel: 01263 732767

For my mother who stood by me
and knew when to detach.

ACKNOWLEDGMENTS

My thanks are abundantly due to Alison, my wife, without whose severe but valuable criticism this work would have been even more imperfect than it is. Numerous colleagues and friends, including Julian Goodacre, Andrew Stilwell, Val Hart, Rosanne Bensley, Anna Magee, Archie Bunce, Steve Roberts, George Forrester, Vajralila, Maggie Noach and Leonard Hook have kindly read the various versions of my manuscript and have offered helpful comments and suggestions. Gloria Ferris and Rivers Scott, my former agents now retired, helped me greatly.

Ilyana Cranston, Steve Goldthorpe and M. Jacques Chevrier, of Chartres, gave me much-needed encouragement in the early stages of this undertaking.

I am especially indebted to my patients (past and present), to my own addictive illness and to Dr Robert Lefever who, between them, have taught me almost everything I know about addiction. Dr Lefever has also suggested numerous improvements to the text and has kindly contributed a Foreword. My sponsees have helped to keep me clean and sober (one day at a time) and I owe an incalculable debt to my three successive Fellowship sponsors.

My greatest debt, however, is to the founders of Alcoholics Anonymous. It is ultimately to their pioneering work that I owe my own recovery – and this book may be regarded as little more than a commentary upon the 12 Step programme of recovery which they gave to the world.

JWRC
Haydon Bridge, April 2006.

TABLE OF CONTENTS

FOREWORD
By Dr Robert M.H. Lefever
Founder of The PROMIS Recovery Centre

Treatment centres are staff-intensive and therefore expensive. Nonetheless, they have a place in helping a larger number of addicts of one kind or another to get into recovery than would otherwise do so. Indeed, that is their only function. Even so, they are not always necessary. Some 'hopeless cases' do get better primarily through working the Twelve Step programme in 'the rooms' (meeting places) of the Anonymous Fellowships such as Alcoholics Anonymous, Narcotics Anonymous and Overeaters Anonymous. John Coats is one such and all credit to him. Even more credit to him for writing this book and reaching out to encourage and help others who could see no end to their recurrent relapses.

Working the Twelve Steps cannot be done alone or by anyone else on our behalf. It has to be done on a day-to-day basis by each of us – on the days when we feel like doing so and also on the days that we do not. It is the persistence that pays dividends. Having a practical guide, as in this book, is helpful but it has to be used as a blueprint for action rather than as an interesting tome to be read and discussed. The Twelve Steps are an action programme or they are nothing.

Similarly, they are a spiritual programme or they are nothing. Addiction is a disease of the human spirit. It eats away at hope, love, trust, honour, innocence and all the beautiful spiritual values that give life its significance. There are physical, mental, emotional, marital, professional, social, economic and all sorts of other consequences (addiction is the most wide-ranging of all conditions in the damage that it can cause). But treating any or all of these consequences still leaves the cause unchecked and ready to wreak havoc again.

A disease of hope, love, trust, honour and innocence has to be treated with hope, love, trust, honour and innocence. That's what the Twelve Steps actually do. And that is what this book bravely attempts to reveal.

Dr Robert Lefever
Director of PROMIS
June 2006

INTRODUCTION

This book is intended primarily for those who know, or suspect, that they have an addictive disorder and who would like to do something about it – without, necessarily, having to go into 'treatment' or 'rehab'. It is not a theoretical work. It is intended to be a practical guide for those who wish to recover from addiction, in any of its many forms.

You will not find any 'definitions' of addiction proposed here. Nor will you find discussion of the different theoretical 'models' of addiction. I wasted too much time, during my own active addiction, speculating about such matters – time which would have been better spent taking action to arrest the progression of my disease.

It is really very simple:

'It's not a problem, unless it's a problem'.

If your addictive behaviours are causing you, or other people, problems in any area of life, it's a good idea to make some changes.

I shall use terms like 'addictive disorder' and 'addictive disease', not because I subscribe wholeheartedly to the so-called 'disease model of addiction', but simply because this approach seems to me to fit best the phenomena which I have observed over more than thirty years. Perhaps more importantly, it is a model which is extremely useful in addressing this condition. Evidence, moreover, continues to mount that there may be an inherited predisposition to addictive/compulsive disorders – that addictive disease is genetic in origin.

Thanks to a number of well-publicised cases, in recent decades, of celebrities who have had problems with addictions, there has been much discussion of the various types of 'treatment' for addiction and of the 'Treatment Centres' and 'Rehabs' where they are offered. As one who is himself in recovery from a number of addictive disorders, and who has been both a patient and a counsellor in some of these treatment centres, I fear that such talk may give rise to a number of misunderstandings.

For there is **no treatment** for addictive disease – at least not in the sense that, say, quinine and its derivatives are treatments for malaria, or insulin for diabetes. If you have an addictive disorder, no wise and benevolent physician can examine and diagnose you and forthwith administer an infallible cure. Nobody can wave a magic wand and 'treat' your condition.

The most that can be done by professionals in the field is to suggest to you ways in which **you can treat your own condition**. Moreover, with all this talk of treatments and of treatment centres, it is often forgotten that for the pioneers of recovery, the 'founding fathers' of Alcoholics Anonymous, there were no such things as 'treatment centres'. They got well under their own steam and with the help of their fellow-sufferers.

Since the early decades of the twentieth century an extraordinary miracle, composed of many smaller miracles, has been occurring. People who would previously have been written-off by the medical/scientific community as 'incurable' addicts or alcoholics have been getting well – and staying well – in significant numbers. Prior to this, most simply died in their addiction. But the strangest aspect of this apparent miracle is that these recoveries have not been brought about through medical, scientific or technological advances. They are not the gifts of material progress. They are the gifts of a bunch of drunks – who claimed that their method was not material, but spiritual.

What was possible for them is certainly still possible for us today.

In the anonymous fellowships throughout the world there are many thousands of people in good recovery who have never seen the inside of a treatment centre. I am not, however, advising anyone *against* going into treatment at a 'treatment centre' or 'rehab'. If you have the financial resources to cover it, it is an excellent idea. In most of them you will be given an intensive introduction to the Twelve-Step Programme of recovery which forms the basis of this book, first elaborated by the founders of Alcoholics Anonymous – and later found to be equally effective in addressing other addictive/compulsive disorders.

But this book is designed primarily for those who, for one reason or another, are unable to go into treatment.

Wealthy people and 'celebrities' do not find it too difficult, usually, to lay their hands on the funds to pay for in-patient treatment. But in the UK public provision for the treatment of addictive disease, though improving, is still pathetic – and private provision is all too often stratospherically expensive.

In the glare of publicity surrounding the drug-taking and drinking of certain celebrities, it is all too easy to forget that the ordinary smoker is also an addict. The man who eats compulsively and the girl who starves herself qualify too. The old lady who cannot get by without her 'nerve tablets' from the doctor almost certainly has addictive disease. Frequent and regular buyers of 'over-the-counter' medications from the chemist would do well to be concerned about their condition. Those who are worried about their sexual compulsions or self-harming will certainly benefit from making some changes. Those who gamble regularly and excessively and those who compulsively try to 'help' or to control others may need to look at their behaviours, their causes and their consequences. Compulsive shopping and overspending are true addictions which may ruin lives. Addictions to internet pornography and to internet gaming are growing concerns. This book is for all of them.

In it, I shall elucidate some of the techniques which are used in treatment centres and discuss how they may be applied in everyday life. The method of recovery suggested here is not the only method possible. But when I did finally begin to get the hang of recovery from my own addictive disorders, it was **not** as an in-patient in a treatment centre. I could no longer afford it. I have no doubt that I benefited from my earlier in-patient treatments. But, for me, the benefits were not durable. I relapsed repeatedly. To find a stable, enduring recovery, I had to start again in the real world. So far, it has worked for me. I believe that it can work for you, too.

Most especially, therefore, this book is also for those who have lost hope of ever getting well: those who may have been through treatment, once or many times, and for whom it does not seem to have 'worked'. It is for people who have come to regard themselves, just as I did, as 'chronic relapsers' – and incapable of changing.

This book is not stuffed full of 'case histories' of patients. This practice, quite apart from being intrusive, can sometimes be little more than a way of filling space. It can also be something of a 'cop-out' by counsellors. Where appropriate, I shall illustrate particular points from my own personal experience of addiction.

For those who are unfamiliar with the terminology of recovery (detox, relapse, fellowship etc.) there is a Glossary of terms at the back of the book.

I should stress that the views expressed in this book are my own. They are based upon my personal and clinical experience. This interpretation of the 12-Step programme of recovery and of the 'Minnesota Method' of treatment should not be taken to represent the 'official' view of any of the anonymous fellowships or of any specific treatment centre.

1.   SOME BASICS

Recovering from any of the different manifestations of addictive disease (alcohol, overeating, undereating, drugs, bulimia, sexual compulsions, compulsive helping or compulsive controlling, compulsive exercising, gambling, risk-taking, shopping, spending etc.) is difficult - and, in the initial stages, it can be very scary indeed.

It demands perseverance, emotional and intellectual honesty and, above all, willingness: willingness to think differently about ourselves and others; willingness to relinquish habits of mind and attitudes which are very deeply embedded. We must somehow become willing and able to change ourselves very fundamentally. We are not speaking here of the superficial 'reinvention' of ourselves regularly practised by actors and 'pop' idols. We do not mean cosmetic 're-packaging'. There is a sense in which we shall have to become new and different people – or at least the people we were meant to be, before addiction warped our lives and distorted our personalities. In most cases, this thorough transformation is not accomplished overnight.

There will never be a time, moreover, when we can say, definitively, that we are 'cured'. In our day to day lives, we shall be able to live in complete freedom from the causes and symptoms of our addictions. But that freedom depends upon active measures to prevent a recurrence of the disorder.

For anyone who knows that he or she has a problem in any of the areas mentioned above, these are some of the realities of recovery. It is as well that, right from the start, we should have no illusions about them. My own first anonymous fellowship 'sponsor' used to say: "There are no Big Deals in recovery". Hence, the title of this book. What he said is true - and the further we progress in recovery, the truer it becomes. Nevertheless, we should never underestimate the difficulties involved in establishing and sustaining a healthy and durable recovery.

If, then, it is so difficult, why bother with recovery? Why not just make 'terms of agreement' with our addictions and try to live with them? For a few unfortunate individuals this *is* possible. They do not usually live happy or fulfilling lives. They do not (usually) live very long. But even someone with, say, a severe addiction to cocaine *can* get by - provided they have an almost inexhaustible supply of cash. They will probably be condemned to a mad, freakish existence of psychosis and paranoia - but they will survive until they die or are killed. For money is not the only thing which is stolen from us by addictive disease. Certainly, it *will* steal our property. But it will also steal less tangible, but more important, things. It will steal our self-respect. It will steal our innocence. It will steal our trustworthiness and our trust in others. It will steal our friendships and other close relationships. It will steal our marriages and our children. It will steal our jobs, our time and our accomplishments. It will steal our true identities. It will steal our enjoyment of our lives - and eventually (left untreated) it will steal our lives themselves. Perhaps, in my own case, the most significant thing it stole from me was my freedom. It stole my freedom to choose, my freedom to act, my freedom to travel, my freedom to create, my freedom to enjoy the company of others, my freedom to take pleasure in this staggeringly beautiful world and all that it contains. It stole my horizons and it stole my dreams. For no matter what I did, or where I went, the ability to satisfy my addictions had to be my first priority. There were even occasions when it stole my physical liberty. Addictive disease does not always obey the Law - and nor did I, while I was under its sway.

Gradually, these things have been restored to me and I *know* that the efforts required by recovery are immeasurably worthwhile. Those little, halting, hesitant efforts are insignificant by comparison with the gifts which recovery confers upon us. When we first embark upon recovery, however, we cannot *know* this. Nothing in our day-to-day experience leads us to suppose that abstinence might have meaningful benefits. So we come face to face with our first difficulty. We have to take it all on trust - and trusting anyone about anything is a practice which most of us have long since discarded. For those who have not yet tasted the blessings of recovery, one of the best ways of assuring ourselves that our trust will **not** be misplaced is to examine the evidence. And one of the best places to look for some of the evidence is at a meeting of one of the 'Anonymous' fellowships (AA, NA, OA, GA, SLAA etc.). And so we come to the first task of this DIY Guide:

ACTIONS   *01.*

(NB If you are already familiar with the Fellowships, do this anyway!)

You do not know it yet – but you are about to visit a website or to make a telephone call which may have a profound and beneficial effect upon your life. You are probably anxious that you might have to reveal your problem to strangers. Don't worry! You don't have to reveal anything at all on the internet or on the telephone. All you need is some basic information.

01. a.   *Find a copy of your local telephone directory or go online.*

01. b   *Look up any of the following (choose the most appropriate):*

> Alcoholics Anonymous
> Narcotics Anonymous
> Overeaters Anonymous
> Gamblers Anonymous
> Nicotine Anonymous
> Sex and Love Addicts Anonymous
> Helpers Anonymous
> Addictions Anonymous
> Debtors Anonymous
> Codependents Anonymous
> Cocaine Anonymous
> Marijuana Anonymous

*Do not worry if you cannot find **exactly** the right Fellowship for you, locally. Choose the one that interests you most. Make a note of the telephone number or find the list of meetings on the website.*

01. c.   *Dial the number and ask **when** and **where** the next local meeting is – or look up your local meetings on the website. Write the information down.*

01. d.   *Go to the meeting. Just do it! You will find there some people who have been in recovery for a number of years – as well as struggling newcomers.*

01. e.   ***Listen** carefully to what the 'old hands' have to say **about themselves** (not about you and not about others).*

2.   LEAVING GOMORRAH BEHIND.

Outside Plaistow underground station, a cold, thin wind probed into every crevice and corner of the brickwork. An emaciated individual sat cross-legged on the pavement clutching a battered guitar. Two strings were missing.

Despite the autumn chill, the man, no longer young, was naked to the waist. Grimy rivulets of sweat trickled down the protruding ribs of his pale, greyish, scrawny chest. Beside him a makeshift placard, crudely fashioned from cardboard and a broom-handle, announced:

BUSKERS' STRIKE
Pay me or...
I PLAY!

Although this dire threat was real enough (his repertoire was limited, his voice atrocious and his playing incompetent), it had apparently failed to intimidate many of the punters. A tattered fur coat lay inside-out on the pavement to his left. The sparse sprinkling of coins that decorated its torn lining suggested that the buskers' strike had not yet brought the country to its knees. All of the coins were of small denominations - and most of them had been strewn there by the busker's own hand some two hours earlier, as an encouragement to passers-by. He stirred the pathetic harvest listlessly with the thin fingers of his left hand.

Not even enough for a drink - let alone cocaine.

And then, in quick succession, two thoughts hit him with astonishing clarity. The first was this: "Only a madman would choose Plaistow Underground as a pitch. What am I doing here?"

There was a pause, vacant and uncertain, before the second thought materialised in his mind. It was this: "There's something not quite right here. I don't know what it is. But *something* has gone horribly wrong. This whole situation is all wrong."

So began my own long, faltering journey away from Gomorrah.

For everyone who suffers from an addictive disorder (involving drink or overeating, drugs or compulsive undereating, sexual compulsions or risk-taking, gambling, spending or compulsive helping, nicotine or compulsive controlling) there is a place which I call Gomorrah - and there are moments when we realise that we're living there. It is the place where our addiction forces us to live. Why Gomorrah? We know very little about the historical city of Gomorrah. We do not even know for certain that it existed. At most we may surmise that it was one of the 'cities of the plain'. Some speculate that it slid beneath the Dead Sea in a great geological upheaval. According to the Book of Genesis, the deeds of its inhabitants provoked the wrath of God and, along with the city of Sodom, it was utterly destroyed. The reputation of Sodom is well-established. But what on earth did they get up to in Gomorrah?

I have found that most addicts have their own Gomorrahs. The details of the landscape may differ - the terrain, the architecture, the inhabitants. But all Gomorrahs have one thing in common. When we are there, we know that we are in the *wrong place*. But Gomorrah is consuming and seductive. It blinds us to this great incongruity. It makes us feel at home. It coils itself, like some great, primeval, serpentine constrictor, stealthily and imperceptibly around our limbs - until we can neither remember nor imagine a life outside its long, duplicitous embrace. It sends phantasms to distract and entertain our minds, while, millimetre by gradual millimetre, it crushes us.

Occasionally, if we are lucky, in a moment of clarity or in a half-remembered dream, we become aware of our true predicament. We understand that a malevolent, creeping power has paralysed, blinded and entombed us. We can see that this base power is taking from us everything that we have ever esteemed. First of all, as we noted in the previous chapter, it takes just money and material things. But then, gradually, it begins to rob us of our values - trust, honesty, courage, enthusiasm, generosity, innocence, hope and joy. It takes away our self-respect and our pleasure in, and respect for, others. It takes away the people we care about and the relationships that are important to us. It takes even our *capacity* to care. Next it steals our health and destroys our sanity. And, finally, sooner or later, one way or another, it robs us of our lives. Tragically, it may also annihilate or damage the people around us. And there is nothing (or so it seems) that we can do to stop it.

All this, at occasional brief moments, we know and can perceive. And at once we thrust the painful, frightening knowledge from us and burrow more deeply into our own Gomorrah's coils. Yet this knowledge is the most important knowledge we can have. It is the only knowledge that can save us and without it we cannot leave Gomorrah behind.

If this chapter has made some sort of sense to you, if you recognise in these descriptions something of your own situation, you are probably one of US. You probably suffer from addictive disease, in one of its many forms. For the sake of convenience, I shall refer to the individual manifestations (excessive gambling, drinking, sex, drugs, starving, gorging, controlling, helping, smoking, spending, exercising etc.) as addictive *disorders*. But these are merely symptoms. Indeed, I have come to regard them as the pitiful ways in which we attempt to *medicate* our underlying condition. Superficially, of course, these behaviours seem to have little in common - apart from the defining qualities of being excessive, mood-altering and having increasingly negative consequences. But years of talking professionally to other addicts have persuaded me that the underlying feelings which give rise to these disparate behaviours – and the ways in which we react to those feelings - are shared by most of us.

It is, therefore, this underlying condition (which I shall call addictive *disease*) that needs to be addressed.

We shall be examining some of its characteristics in the chapters which follow – and we shall be considering some of the ways in which its baneful and ultimately lethal influence upon us can be counteracted.

ACTIONS 02.

N.B. This exercise should always be undertaken under medical supervision.

02. a. *Stop 'medicating' yourself*

Whatever it is that you've been doing to abolish or modify your uncomfortable feelings – stop doing it. This exercise can be difficult and frightening – but it is not a Big Deal. Your addictive disease will probably try to make it a Big Deal – but it isn't.

*If you can get **in-patient** medical supervision during this brief 'detox' (q.v., Glossary), so much the better. This can be arranged through your GP. If not, at least tell your GP what you are intending to do and ask for assistance. You could stop at once and completely - or you could decide upon a gradual, time-limited reduction programme. Both methods have something to be said for them. Discuss with your medical advisor which method would be most appropriate in your case and be prepared to accept this medical advice.*

Except in very rare circumstances, you should aim to be physically free of your substance (drug) or process (gambling, overeating, etc.) of choice in no longer than three weeks. In the case of alcohol and most other drugs, this is relatively straightforward. People who have a long-standing and heavy benzodiazepine addiction may need rather longer. Make a decision to allow yourself to be guided by your medical practitioner. Even if you think that your doctor is misguided and is mishandling your detoxification, submit to the programme recommended. Once you have made this decision, you no longer have to worry about the details of your detox programme. Your energies are freed for the more important work of personal change.

*In the case of eating disorders (anorexia, bulimia, compulsive overeating etc.) 'abstinence' means, quite simply, establishing normal, healthy eating habits. There is much evidence to suggest that the avoidance of 'trigger' foods (usually sugar and other refined carbohydrates) is the key. Seek help with this from other members of an appropriate fellowship or association and, if necessary, from a professional counsellor (see **Actions 03. b**) As with other addictions,* *you cannot begin to make the changes necessary for sustained recovery until you are abstinent from your addictive behaviours.*

Because advanced anorexia can be life-threatening, establishing abstinence (from compulsive starving) should always be undertaken on an in-patient basis.

*For gambling, compulsive helping, sexual compulsions, risk-taking, spending and controlling the same principles apply. In order to achieve simple abstinence from these behaviours you will need to be guided by other members of an appropriate fellowship who are in good recovery – or, if necessary, by a professional counsellor (see **Actions 03. b**) In order to enjoy the benefits of long-term stable recovery, you will need to make some rather more fundamental changes.*

02. b.   *Get emotional support*

During your 'detox' (see Glossary) you will probably be on an emotional rollercoaster ride. This is 'normal'. For years you have been suppressing, abolishing or modifying your feelings by one means or another. Now they will start to come back – and you won't be using your usual techniques for dealing with them. Without these usual techniques, you will probably feel raw, naked and exposed. This can be scary. One moment you may feel euphoric and the next like bursting into tears. No matter how 'hard' you think you are, no matter how well you have controlled and disguised your emotions in the past, no matter how 'embarrassing' it may be, you are going to start having real feelings – and you probably won't know what to do with them.

Here is a suggestion. Try expressing them. Believe it or not, this is what 'normal', healthy people do with their emotions. There are really only two guidelines to observe here:

1.   *Do it in an appropriate way. **Say** how angry you feel. Don't hit someone!*

2.   *Do it in an appropriate context. The check-out girl at Tesco's probably doesn't want to hear about your unhappy childhood. Even if she does seem interested, those behind you in the queue will not appreciate the delay.*

*If you have managed to get yourself into an in-patient detoxification programme (this is **not** the same as 'treatment'), talk to fellow-patients and to some of the professionals who are looking after you.*

*If you are doing a 'home' detox, repeat **Actions 01** on p.15. many times over. Get to as many meetings as you can (most fellowships recommend about 90 meetings in 90 days) - only this time, as well as **listening** to what the others have to say about themselves, start to **talk** about yourself.*

During and after physical detoxification you are likely to experience some very strange and disturbing sensations. These may be physical, psychological or both. Depending on what substances or processes you have been 'using', these may range from the fear that you are about to die, through hallucinations of one kind or another, to physical tremors, convulsions, profuse sweating, sleeplessness, excessive drowsiness, rage, nameless fears, grief and sorrow, hyperactivity, flu-like symptoms, stomach cramps, diarrhoea, nausea and vomiting etc. Physical pains from old injuries etc., which have been masked by drugs, often resurface on detoxification. You will not necessarily get all (or even any) of these signs and symptoms. However, addictive disease does not like being put out of business – and it will do its best to persuade you that you have no alternative but to 'use'.

*It is lying. No matter how bad things may seem, you do **not** have to use.*

*But **do** keep talking. When you experience the phenomenon of craving, phone your sponsor (see Chapter 4), get to a meeting or simply phone a friend in the Fellowship. You will not feel like doing this. You will probably feel like being alone and turning in on yourself. Don't! Keep yourself occupied and turn your attention **outwards**. Clear out the fridge. Go to a movie with fellowship friends. Polish your shoes. Too much introspection at this stage in your recovery will only furnish you with spurious 'justifications' for using.*

*Remember above all that, although these unpleasant feelings may seem to be going on for ever and ever, **they will pass**. Some of them will pass quite quickly, others will gradually diminish over time. This has been the invariable experience of all people who are in recovery. You can depend upon it **absolutely**.*

02. c.   *Be aware of your main 'triggers'*

In some approaches to addiction (especially 'cognitive behavioural' approaches), you are advised to make a list of your 'trigger' situations (situations which, in the past, have 'triggered' episodes of drinking, drugging, bingeing, starving, acting-out sexually, etc.) and to avoid these situations - or to devise new strategies for dealing with them. The simplest illustration of this is that of the alcoholic whose homeward path leads past a favourite 'watering-hole'. He or she is usually advised to find a different route home.

This is not a bad idea. It certainly does us no harm to become more aware of situations which may put us at risk. But it is important to remember three things:

1.   *No list of 'triggers' can ever be comprehensive. We may therefore 'set ourselves up' for a relapse. All too frequently you may hear someone who has recently relapsed say "But seeing my ex-girlfriend (or going to the football match / visiting the in-laws etc.) was not on my list of triggers..."*

2.   *For someone with addictive disease, **any and every** situation may be a trigger because...*

3.   *The real triggers are **not** the external situations. The real triggers are the internal feelings provoked by the situation.*

*We 'use' on our feelings. And **any** feeling will do. It seems to me that one of the most characteristic features of addictive disease is the inability to deal **appropriately** with feelings **of any kind.** Most of us have never learned how to acknowledge, express and resolve our feelings in a healthy way.*

*I know, for instance, that in my own case, when bad feelings arose, I wanted to abolish them immediately – and, of course, the quickest way was to 'use' something: drugs, sex, gambling... anything! But, equally, even when **good** feelings arose, I wanted to prolong, intensify or otherwise modify them – and, again, the best way I knew of doing this was to 'use'.*

*Paradoxically, there are also some people who seem to believe, at some level, that they do not **deserve** to have good feelings. They modify good feelings by 'using' – in order to restore bad (but more familiar) feelings.*

*In theory, therefore, **all** situations may, potentially, be 'trigger' situations – and if we listed them all, the task would never be completed. Nevertheless it is not a bad idea to:*

Make a list of those situations which have most commonly caused you problems in the past.

Divide an A4 sheet of paper into two columns. In the left hand column list, in abbreviated form, the situations which you believe are most likely to lead you to 'use'. In the right hand column say, briefly, how you intend to deal with that situation.

For example:

Situation	**Strategy**
Passing the patisserie	*Take a different route*
Doing a presentation	*Get to know the audience*
'Reward' for hard work	*Relax in a bath instead*
	Etc.

Remember that the aim is not merely to find a mechanical (behavioural) solution to the problem. The aim is to change the way we feel about the situation.

3.   AN ADVANCED CASE

Not long after the incident outside Plaistow Underground station, I had a stroke of great good fortune - although I did not recognise it at the time. Indeed, quite the opposite. I believed that a dreadful fate had overtaken me.

I was shovelled out of a station wagon into the courtyard of a country house in Kent. I had little idea of where I was. The vehicle, I think, belonged to a franciscan friary. I was still wearing the tattered fur-coat. My hair was long and matted, my face consisted mainly of a bushy, unkempt beard. I weighed about seven stone. My battered boots were laced with orange plastic binder-twine from a broken bale of straw. I felt disorientated, extremely unwell and very much alone. I was afraid.

Nurse-type women, in crisp white uniforms, were ushering me into a small outbuilding, asking me endless questions and finally leaving me on a trolley in a little side-room. They said that 'The Doctor' would come and look at me soon... and, for a few moments, I was left in peace.

A kindly looking gentleman with heavy spectacles entered the room. He was tall, thin and slightly stooped. Despite his well-made suit, his cufflinks and his brightly-coloured tie, there was a slightly negligent quality to his appearance - as though he could discern and appreciate excellence but chose to wear it lightly. He was softly spoken, but said very little as he conducted a methodical physical examination. Reflexes. Auscultation. Palpation.

When he had finished he stood beside my trolley and gazed at me levelly and in silence, resting his chin on a raised hand. At last he spoke. His tone was clipped and matter-of-fact:

"Hmm." he said "You're suffering from an advanced case of addictive disease." He turned towards the door. "But we *can* help you.."

And for some reason, I believed him.

I had never previously thought of myself as having a *case* of anything - advanced, incipient or of any other kind. I knew that I behaved and reacted differently from most other people. Sometimes I thought that this was because I was totally inadequate and lacking in some essential faculty - not quite fully human. At other times I theorised absurdly that I must be more highly evolved than most other people - among the first of a new race, the vanguard of *homo superior,* which would soon supplant poor old *homo sapiens.* In the meanwhile, of course, I had to bring myself 'down' to their level by stultifying myself with various chemicals and liquids.

But, in these words spoken by The Doctor, my fuddled brain had recognised another implication altogether. I did not formulate it consciously. I was no longer capable of doing so. But there was a subliminal realisation that The Doctor's words implied that, if I was suffering from a known disease, *others* must have it too. I was not 'terminally unique'. But the thing which ignited a tiny flame of hope, not in my head but in my heart, was this:

Quietly but confidently he spoke about my illness as though it were something very familiar to him - and about which *something could be done.* It was only later that I discovered that 'The Doctor' was himself an addict in recovery.

ACTIONS   03.

Lifestory.

In many treatment centres, one of the first therapeutic exercises that patients are asked to undertake is the **Lifestory.** *This need not be as terrifying as it sounds. Unfortunately, however, the nature and purpose of the exercise are often poorly understood, both by patients and, sometimes, by staff.*

It is **not** *intended to be a blow by blow account of every commendable and discreditable deed which the patient has ever performed. It is* **not** *intended to reveal to you, in a sudden sequence of realisations, the exact nature and causes of your condition. It is* **not** *intended as an act of confession, self-abasement and contrition or to break the haughty spirit of the addict. It does* **not** *need to be punctiliously accurate in matters of fact, chronology and objective truth. It does* **not** *have to be a literary masterpiece. It is* **not** *intended to supply counsellors with a conveniently condensed source of information for their notes.*

The concern that these qualities **may** *be expected can produce a number of different, but equally undesirable, results:*

a)   *The Magnum Opus. The patient writes ream after ream of material, only to find, when it is nearing completion, that an incident (which might be significant) has been omitted from the early pages. The whole document is torn to shreds. With painstaking perseverance the labour is recommenced.*

b)   *The Invisible Lifestory. The patient believes that they are unequal to the task. "I'm too stupid" "I can't spell properly" "I can't think straight" "I can't remember anything" "I can't do it properly, so I'm not going to do it at all".*

c)   *The Press Release. This is the 'official version', designed to create the right impression; carefully crafted, meticulously sanitised and heavily bowdlerised. It is a rationalisation. It attempts to explain the inexplicable and to justify the unjustifiable.*

There are many other types of Lifestory presented: the 'Abject Apology', the 'Gripping Yarn', the 'Slight Exaggeration', the 'I've

Never had a Break from all those Bastards', the 'I'm So Boring and Ordinary' etc. All of them miss the point. All too often, alas, the point is missed quite simply because staff in treatment centres have failed to explain that the Lifestory exercise is mainly for the benefit of the writer, not for the benefit of the counsellors or of the Group. It has three main functions:

1. *It is intended to help you to* **begin** *to get a better perspective on your life and on what has been happening to you*

2. *It is intended to help you to* **begin** *to be able to trust others, to risk some small self-disclosures and to share your experiences with other human beings*

3. *It is intended to give a group of fellow human beings a rough idea of the patient's personality, where they are 'coming from' and where they are at now. Without these, the group will not be able to help.*

Provided the lifestory exercise serves these three basic purposes, this is all that is required.

03. a.   Write your lifestory

This is a good exercise to perform, whether you are in treatment or not. Bearing in mind the above points, do it in whatever manner suits you best. You can write it all out consecutively, word for word, or you can simply make a list of headings which remind you of particular events. Try to keep it 'unadorned' (e.g. "In 1997 my children were taken away from me" **not** *"In 1997 my bastard husband lied in Court until he was blue in the face and that moronic judge ordered my children to be taken away... ").*

03. b.   Talk it through with at least one other person.

The main disadvantage of embarking on recovery without in-patient treatment is that you do not have a resident, ready-made group of fellows in early recovery. You can compensate for this in very large *measure by regular attendance at fellowship meetings, where there will be people who understand what you are trying to do. You can also, of course, see a counsellor on a regular basis. Choose one, preferably, who offers **group** therapy sessions. You may not be able to do this entirely for free. But it will certainly be a great deal less expensive than residential treatment.*

Most of us would rather have 1/1 counselling than group therapy. This is because we find it easier to manipulate a single counsellor than a room full of people like us. We may also shrink from disclosing the significant facts of our experience and our true feelings about them to comparative strangers. This is to be expected. Secrecy and surreptitiousness are the stock-in-trade of addictive disease. Nevertheless, more than anything else, it is our authentic contact with other people which will eventually heal the scars and distortions of addictive disease. The sooner, therefore, that we can bring ourselves to begin to communicate honestly and openly with our fellow human beings, the sooner the healing process will begin.

03. c.   Offer to do a 'chair' or 'share' at one of your regular fellowship Meetings.

*Use your notes as the basis for what you will say. The first time you do this can be very nerve-wracking indeed. Tell the meeting that it is your first 'chair' and that you are very nervous. They **will** be very supportive. The old-hands will remember their own terror in early recovery. The novices will admire your courage.*

One of the most positive things you can do at this stage of your recovery is to find a fellowship Sponsor. This will be explained in the next chapter.

4. POLICE CELLS AND LUNATIC ASYLUMS

I would like to be able to tell you that, having arrived at the Treatment Centre in Kent, I immediately got well and recovered from the multiple addictions which had brought me to destitution. It would not be true. Nor was this the first time that I had undergone 'treatment' of one sort or another.

In addition to numerous admissions to psychiatric hospitals, numerous detoxifications, manifold and multiform attempts to treat, control or 'cure' my inveterate, self-destructive compulsions, I had also already been in a well-known 'Twelve Step' Treatment Centre in Wiltshire. Sooner or later (but usually sooner) I reverted to my former habits - or *relapsed*, as they say in the network.

Nor was this to be the last time that I would find myself a patient in the country house in Kent. I was to have two further admissions before I finally began to get the hang of it. My own disorders were peculiarly tenacious - and I was unusually obstinate in clinging to the belief that I would prove to be different from others. It might be advisable for *them* to abstain from all mood-altering substances and processes - but I was more spiritual than they, more intelligent, better able to learn how to *master* this thing. I cannot now recommend this attitude. It cost me a number of wasted years. It caused a great deal of unnecessary suffering to those who were close to me. It ensured that my own deterioration, mental, physical and spiritual, became even more 'advanced' than it was when The Doctor had first seen me. And each relapse was worse than the last.

In the active phase of my addictive disorder, between the ages of 15 and 40, I kept ending up in police cells, in hospitals and in lunatic asylums. As I sit and write these words, I am in my fourteenth year of recovery from active addiction. During all those years I have never yet been obliged to reside in any of the above types of accommodation. This, I sometimes venture to think, cannot be a coincidence.

It is my hope that many who read this book will be more astute and less obstinate than I was – that they will not yet have allowed their addictive disease to progress as far as mine unfortunately did. By the same token, I am sure that there will be many whose experience of this disease has been more catastrophic than mine – who may have been permanently disabled or who have ended up in psychiatric institutions or prisons for long periods of time. None of us, however, should have any illusions. If addictive disease is allowed to run its course untreated, sooner or later, by one means or another, directly or indirectly, it will kill us. Through accidents or through incidental illnesses, through its own physically destructive effects or through their consequences, by fires, by depression and suicide, by toxicity and poisoning, by damage to liver, kidneys, brain, lungs or pancreas, in road traffic accidents or by falling downstairs, by malnutrition or by choking on our own vomit, by overdose, suffocation or by violence; one way or another it will get us. It is versatile. It is patient. It is subterranean. It is fatal.

Some may say "Don't be daft. How can behaviours such as overspending, or overexercising or compulsive helping kill a person?" There are three answers to this. Firstly, long before destroying us physically, they will destroy our quality of life. They will vitiate our relationships, wreck our work and imperil our bank-balances. Secondly, the addictive disease which underlies these behaviours, left untreated, will continue to progress. Our mood will be increasingly affected. Our sanity will be increasingly impaired. Thirdly and finally, there are very few people who suffer from one form of addictive disease who are not susceptible to other forms. Over time, we tend to 'cross-addict'. During the course of my own recovery from addiction to drugs and alcohol, I have had problems with cigarette-smoking, with 'over-the-counter' medications, with gambling and with certain types of relationship. With the help of some of my fellows in recovery, I have been able to identify these problems and to take appropriate action.

The idea, therefore, that addictive disease is relatively harmless, and nothing to make a fuss about, is a dangerous delusion. The only thing which benefits from this delusion is the disease itself. As long as we can persuade ourselves, either that we haven't got it, or that, even if we *have* got it, it's not really serious, the disease can continue to flourish – and our lives will continue to deteriorate. It is often said that this is the only disease that tells you that you haven't got it.

But there is another delusion, from which I also suffered for many years, which is almost equally an enemy to recovery. We may be in no doubt that there is something profoundly wrong with us. We may even accept that we have addictive disease. We may even have tried to do something about it. Perhaps we have tried various 'cures'. Perhaps we have been through a residential 12-Step treatment programme – once or many times. And yet, we have repeatedly found ourselves back at 'square one'. We have 'relapsed'. We have suddenly realised that the brakeless juggernaut of addiction has careered away with us again and has dumped us (if we were lucky enough not to fall and be crushed) stupefied, uncomprehending, perplexed and despairing in places we never wanted to end up. Again and again.

For some of us this happened so often that we came to regard ourselves as 'chronic relapsers': people for whom the recovery programme simply 'didn't work' - and probably never would. Perhaps we were the 'unfortunates' (referred to in the AA Big Book) who were 'constitutionally incapable of being honest with themselves'.

Or were we outstandingly stupid? It certainly looked that way. We had been doing the same sort of things, over and over again. Why, unless we were very, very stupid, should we be surprised that the results were always the same, too? The consequences of our actions were repeatedly disastrous - if anything, they got worse each time. How could we forget these glaring facts so quickly?

Might it be true, after all, that we simply had less 'will-power' than other people? Less, even, than our fellow addicts and alcoholics?

Many of us started to believe these unflattering ideas. We strongly suspected and feared that it might all be true. We were just inadequate people - deficient in some fundamental way that we would never know. Not quite fully human - and therefore doomed.

So, of course, it followed that there was no point in battling on. We might as well give up and accept our fate. We might as well lead our brief lives enslaved to our addiction - until it killed us. It couldn't be helped. *We* couldn't be helped. So ran our melodramatic and faulty reasoning.

One of the most characteristic features of this condition is that it involves, not just a disorder of mood, but also a disorder of *perception*. Quite often, our *perception* of a situation simply does not correspond to the realities of that situation, as they are perceived by others. To remain sane we need constantly to check our reality with our fellows. We have only to call to mind the occasions during active addiction when we have chosen to follow our own impulses, in opposition to the advice of those around us, to see that it has usually proved disastrous. And yet we persist with this insane practice!

However, this second delusion (that our repeated failures signify that we have no control over the ravages of our addiction and that there is therefore no hope for us) is more subtle than the first delusion (that there is nothing much wrong with us).

The *first* part of this proposition - that we have no control over our addiction - is completely true, as we shall see in the chapters which follow. It is the *second* part (that there is therefore neither hope nor help for us) that is simply self-pitying piffle, slyly appended by our addictive disease. It does not stand up to scrutiny. Certainly, we have demonstrated that, whenever we follow our own counsels, we seem to get into difficulties. We do not seem to be able to help *ourselves*.

But there are hundreds of thousands of delightful people who *can* help us very effectively. They are people like us who, *somehow*, have found a solution to these same problems. But they can only help us **if we can bring ourselves to ask for their help - and if we are prepared to listen to our fellows and to *act upon* what they say to us.**

ACTIONS   *04.*

Recollection and asking for help.

04. a.   *Think of all the people you have known about who have died while still in active addiction. How many of them died of 'natural' causes – causes unrelated to their addictive illness?*

04. b.   **Get a Sponsor.**

In the Anonymous Fellowships, a Sponsor is someone, of the same gender as you (unless you are gay), who has been in sustained recovery for longer than you and who is able to help you with your own programme of recovery. A sponsor does not charge you for this help.

What should I look for in a person who may become my Sponsor?

The answer to this question will depend very largely upon the **type** *of recovery you want for yourself. For the most part, this is common sense. If you would like to be (as the AA 'Big Book' says) 'happy, joyous and free', then it makes sense to look for someone who exhibits those qualities - and to find out what they are doing which enables them to live that way. It's no good going to some up-tight, miserable, angst-ridden old bastard and expecting to learn how to acquire the qualities you want. We cannot give to others what we do not have ourselves. The same principle, incidentally, may be useful in our choice of professional counsellors.*

If, on the other hand, you're not really comfortable unless you've got something to be anxious, depressed and distraught about, then by all means find a miserable old bastard as your sponsor. He or she will almost certainly be able to help you to become even more miserable than you already are. Early in my own recovery I used to go to what were then called 'Joys of Recovery' meetings. And although, today, I have certain reservations about this type of approach for some newcomers, they did teach me one thing which I believe is ultimately true. "Misery" they said "is optional". Short term pain – transient misery – is, I believe, inescapable. But misery as a long-term, habitual state is certainly optional.

Apart from these personal qualities, then, what else should you look for in your prospective sponsor? Again, this is mostly common sense. They should have been abstinent for a considerable period of time. After all, if they have managed to remain at least abstinent, they must be doing something right.

And, finally, I would suggest that it is a good idea to find a sponsor who gets to meetings regularly and who talks about the Steps (the 12 Step Programme of Recovery, which underpins all of the anonymous fellowships). If our sponsors are to help us with our recovery, then it is reasonable to expect that they should be familiar with (and practising) their own programme. A good indication of this can sometimes be gained from whether or not your sponsor talks much about their own sponsor.

*If they don't – or if they don't **have** a sponsor – be very wary.*

Most of us, left to our own devices, become seriously deranged!

Exactly how do I 'get a sponsor' ?

1.   *Go to a meeting*
2.   *Choose someone with whom there is no possibility of a romantic or sexual entanglement, who seems to make sense to you - and who has some of the characteristics mentioned above*
3.   *Ask that person to be your temporary sponsor*

If they are qualified and do not have too many other commitments, they will agree. If for some reason they can't, they may refer you to someone else – or you could simply choose someone else. If a prospective sponsor says no, do not take it personally. If necessary, go on doing this until you have equipped yourself with a temporary sponsor. It is better to have a temporary sponsor than no sponsor at all.

Now you are abstinent, you have got a temporary sponsor and you can relax... a bit. There will be plenty of time to look for a permanent sponsor – or you may find that your temporary sponsor is just fine and ultimately becomes your permanent sponsor. In any case, there is someone to whom you can turn with your perplexities. Exchange telephone numbers with your new sponsor.

Whether we are feeling perplexed or not, it is a good idea, in early recovery, to get into the habit of having contact with our sponsor, either by telephone or in person, every day. Make sure you set aside 10-20 minutes of private time each day for this purpose. Even if you are not having any particular problems, 'check-in' with your sponsor. Extraordinary though it may seem to you, your sponsor will appreciate the call. Every good sponsor knows that, paradoxically, where recovery is concerned, we can only keep what we have by continually giving it away. Your sponsor's own recovery is strengthened by helping you.

5.   SETTING OUT.

"Oh, God!" says The Voice in my head "Do I really need to go today? I'm exhausted. My brain has packed up. I won't be able to pay attention. Besides, I've heard it all a million times before - all those dreary fanatics, droning on about their dreary little lives, their bloody 'Programme' and their ghastly 'Steps'. Trying to outdo each other with their grisly 'war-stories'. They're all such hypocrites, anyway.

"I bumped into that Julia last week at the station - and she was completely mashed. Zoppo. Out of her head on something or other. I'm not surprised. That idiot Charlie's been trying to get into her knickers for the last three weeks - ever since Mandy turned him down. He thinks the Fellowship is just a dating agency. And *he's* been around for years! They're **all** a bunch of wankers.

"I'd be better advised to finish off some of my work. Or just to get some rest. I certainly need it. I'm weary, weary, weary. I just need to veg out in front of the telly for a couple of hours. Something mindless... not too demanding. Then off to bed. I'm half asleep, as it is..."

This is a fairly typical example of the kind of internal monologue that passes through my mind after a hard day's work, when I know that I ought to get along to one of my regular Fellowship meetings. Pretty convincing, isn't it? Well-marshalled arguments, ably supported by carefully nurtured feelings of resentment and disillusionment, all tending inexorably to the desired conclusion: perhaps I could skip the meeting (just this once). After all, I've been in recovery for quite a long time now. Surely I don't have to go to *quite* so many meetings? One missed meeting is not going to matter very much.

It's all very plausible. There is only one problem. Whose voice is telling me all this?

It can't be my rational, observant, analytical self. How do I know this? Well, because, if I stop to think about it, the objective facts of the case are rather different from the picture presented by The Voice.

In reality, there are almost no fanatics at the meetings I attend. The majority of the people there are charming, modest, sincere and thoughtful people. They do not lead dreary lives. Many of them have lives which are a great deal more colourful and entertaining than my own. Only very rarely are there instances of vying with each other to be 'war-story' laureate. Occasionally there **is** odd behaviour by one member or another. Of course! In any random group of people, there will be one or two who behave oddly from time to time. Thank God. Besides, one of the purposes of the Fellowship is that we help each other with our various oddities. The truth is that, each time I go to a meeting (once I get there) I enjoy it enormously. I meet my chums. We have a good laugh. I invariably learn something new. There is never any lack of interesting or entertaining conversation – if I can be bothered to find it. It is a huge relief to be among people who understand what I'm talking about - because they think, react and function like me. I usually leave the meeting feeling encouraged and uplifted. And yet, the very next time I am supposed to be going to a meeting, The Voice cuts in with its dreadful, specious, plausible drivel. Baldly and boldly, it is telling me lies!

For me, there is really only one explanation. The Voice which I am hearing is the voice of my disease. And if the voice of my disease is so loud and persuasive, I certainly need to get to a meeting!

"What do you get" runs one of the quips sometimes heard among people in recovery from addictive disease "if you dry out a drunken horse-thief?"

Answer: "A thirsty horse-thief!"

The point here is that mere abstinence from your substance or process of addiction is not enough. Separating people from their drink, drugs, food, sex, gambling etc. is only the **first** of the tasks which face professionals who work with addictive disease. In many senses, it is the simplest part of the process. It may be frightening, uncomfortable and painful for the patient - but it is merely a technical matter. Provided the potential risks (convulsions, hallucinations, suicidal tendencies, psychotic episodes etc.) are properly managed, mere abstinence is relatively simple to achieve.

However, a thirsty horse-thief will probably continue to steal horses – and a thirsty person who steals horses will probably start drinking again. **Do not, therefore, be deceived into thinking that programmes which offer nothing more than detoxification (in from five days to several months) are in any sense an adequate 'treatment' for addiction**. Detoxification (the physical separation of the individual from their substances or processes of choice) is only and exactly what it says it is. It is a preliminary, physical, measure which makes *possible* the much more fundamental personal changes which will be needed. If we leave treatment fundamentally the same people as we were when we entered treatment, there is a very strong likelihood that, sooner or later, we shall end up doing the same kind of things. Recovery, I repeat therefore, is all about change – profound, thoroughgoing, radical, personal change.

Detoxification is, however, a *necessary* condition for embarking upon recovery. We **cannot** work a programme of recovery while we are still using. Believe me. I tried it many times!

One reason for this is very simple and has already been mentioned. Addictive disease involves not only a distortion of our emotions, but also of our *perceptions*. As long as we continue to use mood-altering substances or processes, our perceptions of ourselves and of others, of our motives, values, actions and intentions will remain faulty and distorted. Indeed, they remain pretty faulty and distorted, even *after* we have become abstinent. Look at the drivel (at the beginning of this chapter) which my addictive disease still feeds me, fourteen years on, when I ought to be getting to a meeting! Gradually, over time, I have *begun* to be able to recognise this tripe for what it is - sick talk. It's relatively easy to spot it in other people, much more difficult to discern it in ourselves. For this reason it is important for me to take regular and frequent 'reality checks' with other people who are in recovery. They may not be able to spot their own bullshit; but they're not bad at pinpointing mine. And I can usually return the favour!

If you are one of the people who is similar to me in this respect, it might not be a bad idea for you to perform frequent and regular 'reality checks', too, with other people who are in recovery. It could save you from having to learn 'the hard way'.

Another reason why we cannot work a fully effective programme of recovery while we are still using mood-altering substances or processes is that much of the work required must be done at a deep and authentic emotional level. While our emotions are 'blocked' with drugs etc., we cannot work effectively at this level. Sometimes, where there is concurrent psychiatric illness, it may be necessary to continue psychiatric medications. But a surprising proportion of patients who arrive in treatment with all manner of dire and dreadful psychiatric diagnoses *do* get well and stay well (without psychiatric medication) once they have been separated from their drugs for a time - and have embarked upon a programme of recovery. Much long-term psychosis is actually caused by drugs, illegally acquired or legally prescribed.

Addictive disease, moreover, does not distinguish between drugs which are prescribed and those which aren't. It doesn't care whether they are legal or illegal. As long they're mood-altering they'll do just fine. We should not imagine, therefore, that we don't have a problem, just because we are using a respectable doctor as our 'dealer'.

It goes without saying, however, that psychiatric medications should not be stopped suddenly and should only be discontinued under medical supervision.

In order to achieve and sustain our **recovery** from addictive disease we must arrive at a number of consecutive points where:
a) we want our recovery
b) we want it **more** than we want our present, addictive life
c) we recognise that there is no realistic alternative to recovery

In my own case, it took a very long time to arrive there. Even during the later active phases of my own addictive disorders, I wanted recovery – in a theoretical way. But I did not truly believe that recovery was possible for me. It might be for others. But I was rightly convinced that I did not have what it took. None of us, unaided, do.

Nor did I want it *more* than I wanted to continue using. It was not until the 'balance of pain' had shifted further that I began to realise that the only realistic alternative to recovery was death. And death was something I didn't want (most of the time). For me, and for many like me, it was not until the pain of continuing in active addiction exceeded the inescapable pain of starting on the road to wholeness, that recovery became a realistic option to be considered.

For many of us, this shift in 'the balance of pain' has often taken place long before our denial-systems will allow us to acknowledge it. Our addictions are causing us (and many others) extreme misery. But we are not yet ready to admit it. Our addictive disease succeeds in keeping us sick.

The observant reader will have noticed that I have frequently referred to addictive disease as though it were a malevolent personality, in some way separate from my 'real' self. A great deal of nonsense is spouted by a large number of people involved in the 'therapy industry'.

It is an industry laden with untested hypotheses and permeated with unexamined assumptions. I have been surprised to learn, for instance, that all manner of beings dwell within me – an Inner Hero, an Inner Child, an Inner Wolf, an Inner Warrior, an Inner Wizard, an Inner Jester etc., etc. It's getting pretty crowded in there and I have no wish to add my addictive disease to this wailing, jabbering, howling throng. It should be understood, therefore, that this personification of the illness is, of course, only a metaphor. It is a convenient metaphor and there is some psychological truth in it. But it is not wholly accurate in any final, empirical sense.

Human personality is extremely complex. In our attitudes, in particular, there may often be ambivalence. A single individual may display attitudes which are not merely inconsistent, but downright contradictory. This is especially the case for most of those who contemplate recovery from addictive disease.

For most of us, when we first begin to consider the possibility of changing our whole manner of living, it is not a very attractive proposition. Perhaps a small part of us does not wish to continue living as we have been, our every waking moment dominated by our need to 'use'. Certainly, very few of us wish to continue living with the *consequences* of our addiction; the fractured relationships with spouses, parents, children; the disgust of former friends and colleagues; the lies and the dishonesties; the financial chaos; the damaged health, the fear. But nor do we want to do what we know we have to do, to begin to repair our lives. We usually conceive of the task as 'giving up' the substance or process upon which we have come to rely. And we are scared.

It is not easy, however, to admit (even to ourselves) that we are scared. And, of course, the best way we know of abolishing the fear (at least temporarily) is to use - drink, overeat, starve, shop, have sex, gamble – whatever.

The essential dichotomy is this. When we first adopt our substance or process of choice, we do so because it seems to help us to cope. It replaces the bad feelings of anger, inadequacy, fear, shame, guilt, alienation etc. with other, more acceptable feelings. So we come to regard it as our friend, our support, our saviour in all the difficulties, dangers and vicissitudes of life.

And to this friend we are very loyal. We do not *want* to believe that, all the time, it has been undermining us, cheating us, telling us lies, luring us into places we never wanted to go. Nor do we want to admit that this friend, this help, this support has now become our master – that it has now become indispensable to us and that we would do almost anything, no matter how base, in its service. We hide from these facts and we hide these facts from ourselves. We pretend to ourselves that we are still in control. We may even manage to abstain – for a while. And we say "See? I can give it up any time!". But we always go back to our 'friend'. Why *should* we give up our only *real, reliable* friend? Most of the people we thought were our friends are deserting us, one by one – because of our deteriorating behaviours. But this, our only 'true' friend, can be relied upon to do what it has always done – to make us *feel* better; or at least not quite so bad… for a time.

We choose, therefore, to ignore the fact that, not only are the bad feelings, which our friend promised to abolish, still there most of the time, but they have got very much worse. As a result of our relationship with our 'friend' we now feel even more angry and inadequate, we have new sources of shame and guilt, new and terrible fears – and our sense of loneliness and alienation is more profound than ever. Our refusal to recognise this connection between our addiction and all the bad things which are happening in our lives is, of course, called '**denial**'. It is this denial which blinds us to the fact that the 'balance of pain' has already shifted and which prevents us from:

a) wanting our recovery

b) wanting it **more** than we want our present, addictive life

c) recognising that there is no realistic alternative to recovery.

ACTIONS   05.

05. a.   **Divide an A4 sheet of paper into two columns. In the left hand column list all the bad things in your life at present. In the right hand column list all the good things, thus:**

BAD   **GOOD**

Unable to pay my bills   *My wife/husband is still with me*
                                                              Etc.

05. b.   **How many of the good things in your life do you owe to your addictive disorder?**
            Count the number, from your list, and write it below.

                              ....

05. c.   **How many of the bad things in your life do you owe to your addictive disorder?**
            Write the number below.

                              ....

05. d.   **Reflection.**

Is your substance/process of choice still a good 'friend' to you?

6. LOOKING BEHIND THE SCREEN – STEP ONE

I have indicated elsewhere that, to some of us, **in-patient** treatment may **not** be of much immediate benefit – if we are not ready for it. It may be better for us to pursue our recovery in the outside world. Back in 1988, a couple of years prior to my arrival at the treatment centre in Kent, I had been a patient in another well-known treatment centre in Wiltshire. I had gone there because I was at that time involved in a strange kind of relationship with a woman who was very keen on recovery – and I wanted to impress her.

On arrival at the treatment centre in Wiltshire I was, at first, very obstreperous. The regime in the treatment centre was fairly strict and, being rebellious by nature, I found it difficult to submit to rules and regulations whose purpose was obscure to me. We had to sleep in dormitories. We were not allowed any music or TV. For the first seven days we were allowed neither visitors nor telephone calls. They confiscated all my books – and we were only permitted to read material connected with the recovery programme and supplied by 'them'. The daily routine began early in the morning and consisted of household duties (which, for some reason, they called 'therapeutic duties'), group therapy sessions, written exercises, more groups, brief meals, 'therapeutic' washing-up, more groups, videos, groups again, lectures and yet more groups. Even our appearances, our hairstyles and the way we dressed, were governed by others.

"You're trying to dehumanise us!" I protested indignantly, during one of my early group-therapy sessions.

"No, John." replied the counsellor facilitating, with a weary sigh "We're trying to *re*-humanise you."

The belief that we have choices and are ultimately in control of our own destinies is very important to most human beings. It is, for the most part, a justifiable belief. But when we are in the grip of active addiction the power of choice is taken from us. Let me illustrate this by telling you what happened in the weeks and months after the group in which I protested about 'dehumanisation'.

I decided, reluctantly, that I was going to conform. I did everything that was asked of me. I completed all the written exercises. I participated actively in groups. I spoke of events in my life which I had never disclosed to anybody. I went through treatment with gritted teeth, grimly determined to succeed. I hated every minute of it.

Then, right at the end of my treatment, the counsellors decided that, after primary treatment, I would do well to go into a 'halfway house' for several months of secondary treatment. This was too much. When I disagreed, they said I should "take it to the Group". I tried, therefore, to 'knobble' every member of my group. One by one, I accosted them in dark corners of the treatment centre and told them what these inhuman counsellors were proposing. It was outrageous, they said. It was preposterous. I had done so well! I had worked so hard. They did not think that I needed secondary treatment. I was delighted! I was confident that, when the question arose for discussion in group, I would have the support of all my peers – that I would **not** be advised to commit myself to further months of treatment in a halfway house. I felt satisfied with the successful manipulation I had performed.

But something terrible happened. Although, individually, they had all agreed with me that I was ready to leave treatment and go back into the world, when I raised the topic in group, they all said the opposite. They said I should go to the halfway house! Naturally, I felt betrayed and angry. I suspected a conspiracy.

I was wrong. I now know that their change of attitude was not prearranged. It was simply the power of the group at work. They could see, as a group, what they could not see as isolated individuals – that I was not ready. Or at any rate the security of the group allowed them to say what they really felt.

I went, very resentfully, to the halfway house. I was certain that it was completely unnecessary. I was certain that my drinking and drugging days were over. Primary treatment, I thought, had furnished me with all the skills and all the insights I needed to remain clean and sober and to begin to enjoy the benefits of recovery. After two and a half weeks in secondary care, I decided, unilaterally, that it was more important "for my recovery" to go and sort out my relationship with the woman who had guided me into treatment. I rose early one morning, before the others were awake, and caught the train to London. By the time I stepped off the train I was legless with drink. By the evening, my bloodstream carried a cocktail of drugs. I had sincerely believed that this relationship would be good for my recovery. But my pursuit of it had reawakened my addictive disease. It had been part of my addiction.

There was also a rather crucial factor which I had decided to overlook in all this. The woman whom I was pursuing was another man's wife. I should not have been messing around with her in the first place. Needless to say, the relationship didn't work out – but a lot of people got hurt.

It was a long time before I remembered the parting words of my counsellor at the treatment centre, on the day I had graduated from treatment. "Remember, John" he had said "the Fellowships are your lifeline". He had obviously recognised that, despite my apparently exemplary completion of treatment, I was heading for a relapse.

The First Step of the programme of recovery elaborated by the 'founding fathers' of AA was this:
'We admitted we were powerless over alcohol – that our lives had become unmanageable.'

For the present purposes there is absolutely no need to change any of the essentials of this programme. Many people have tried to 'improve' upon the original programme of recovery. Most people who take the trouble to work through the programme come to realise that such attempts are not only arrogant and misguided – they are usually also notably unsuccessful. The reformulated programmes don't seem to work very well. However, we do know, now, that it is not only alcohol and alcoholism that can be successfully treated by the Twelve Step programme. It is every form of addictive disorder. In the light of this knowledge let us, therefore, substitute 'our condition' for the word 'alcohol', thus:

Step One:
We admitted that we were powerless over our condition and that our lives had become unmanageable.

What exactly do we mean by this?

Note the first word. There is a universe of meaning in this one word 'we'. The world of active addiction is an intensely private and secretive world. We would not want most people to know the things we are driven to do by our illness. Often, we think that we are the only people in the world who do these disgusting, inexplicable things. Many of the specific actions involved in practising and sustaining our process of addiction are carefully hidden from others. Usually we also try to hide them from ourselves. We try to explain them away as necessary in a way that other people might not understand. This belief that nobody else could possibly understand our behaviours may sometimes lead us to despair. It almost always prevents us from seeking help.

To most of us, it comes as a huge relief to find that, not only are there many other people who understand perfectly our own bizarre actions and reasonings but that these people have themselves engaged in the same actions and reasonings. Our illness has led us into increasing isolation. Our healing (our re-humanisation) takes place through the company and society of our fellows.

Let us turn now to the rather frightening word 'admitted'. To **admit** that we are powerless over anything (especially our addictive process) is the last thing most of us want to do. Sometimes, if it suits our purposes, we may give lip-service to this idea when we are speaking to others. But we do **not** like to admit *to ourselves* the complete loss of control over our own actions which this implies. We console ourselves with various delusions. "I could stop it if I *really* wanted to." "I can stop it if I really *have to*." "I can easily cut it down." "I could easily stop it for a while." etc., etc.

I have come to think of Step One as primarily a 'denial-busting' step. **Until we look at a thing, we cannot see it.**

Until we dare to look squarely and honestly at the realities of our addiction, we cannot see the havoc of our lives. Until we acknowledge these realities *to ourselves*, we will do nothing about them. You may have noticed that this chapter is called **Looking Behind The Screen.** Sometimes, if there is something unsightly in our living-room, we put up a screen in front of it, to hide it. It is still there, of course, but neither we nor our visitors can see it. The unfortunate truth is that most of us erect a mental screen to hide the realities of our addiction *from ourselves* as well as from others.

When patients in most 12 Step treatment centres start to work on Step One, they are usually given a worksheet which asks them to give as many *specific examples* of their 'powerlessness and unmanageability' as possible. This can be confusing. During my first treatment, as a patient in Wiltshire, I had little idea of what was meant by these rather abstract ideas. If we break them down into their component parts, however, it becomes much more simple. What might it mean, if we said that we were 'powerless' over something? King Canute (Knut) is said to have demonstrated, by empirical experiment, to himself and to his court, that there were limits to his power: that he was powerless, for instance, to prevent the tide from rolling in. It is a fairly simple experiment. You might like to try it yourself.

Go to the seaside on a calm sunny day. Choose a shallow tidal area, when the tide is out. If you happen to have access to an imposing-looking throne, place it on the flat sand directly in the path of the incoming tide. If no throne is available, a deck-chair will serve. Be seated. Place your bare feet upon the sand in front of you – and do not move them. Sitting upon your chosen seat, summon up every ounce of authority and of will-power that you can find within yourself and *command* the sea to stay where it is. *Will* it not to advance towards you. Shout and bellow at it, if you like. To be fair to the sea, you must stay there until it would normally have reached the place where you are sitting. If a tiny wavelet touches your toes, the experiment is over.

The nice thing about this experiment is that, no matter what the outcome may be, you are to be congratulated. The experiment is always a success. If the sea stays put and does not advance, you have demonstrated that you have superhuman powers which are, at present, inexplicable in scientific terms – and that you are a better human being than King Canute. If your feet get wet, you have demonstrated that there are certain forces over which you personally have no control whatever. Addiction is one of them.

There is no shame in this. Should we be ashamed that we cannot personally control the forces of nature – the hurricane, the tornado or the tides? Should a person born with a genetically inherited illness, say haemophilia or cystic fibrosis, feel ashamed of this fact? Of course not. The evidence is mounting that this is precisely the case with addictive illness. It would seem to be related to an inherited deficiency in the neurotransmission functions of the brain.

As we shall see in Chapters 9, 13 and 14, this does **not** absolve us from accountability for the actions which have resulted from our addiction. However, any process over which we have no control is, by definition, unmanageable. Addictive illness eventually permeates every aspect of our lives. It is not altogether surprising, therefore, that, as the illness progresses, our lives become progressively more and more unmanageable. Let's look at the evidence. Let's look behind the screen.

ACTIONS   *06.*

We need to ask ourselves a number of searching questions. And we need to answer them honestly. We need to look at our behaviour as objectively as possible and to examine the unadorned facts – without glosses, without excuses, without rationalisations, without self-justification. It will help us to be as specific as possible.

Below are some questions relating to incidents from our recent or more distant past. I would suggest that, as we look at these events, we consider each one from the following points of view:

> *When did it happen?*
> *Where did it happen?*
> *Who was involved?*
> *What, exactly, did happen?*
> *What were the consequences for me?*
> *What were the consequences for other people?*

*Remember that we are looking only at **our own** behaviour. Other people involved may have behaved well or badly. It does not matter. We are not interested in them at present. We are only interested in what we ourselves **did**. We are not even particularly interested in what we may have been thinking or feeling at the time. We are going to look at our **actions**. Write down, on paper, your answers to the following questions:*

Questions 06. a. and 06. b., below, relate to our loss of control over our using.

06. a.   Have I, at any time, resolved not to engage in my addictive behaviour (drinking, smoking, injecting, snorting, starving, overeating etc., etc.) – but found that I was unable to carry out this resolve?

A simple "yes" in answer to this question is not enough. Your mind will probably recoil from looking at the number of times it has happened and at the precise details of what happened. Your mind, in other words, will try to put up the screen. But you need to answer the questions above (When? Where? Who? What? etc.) in order to begin to get a just appreciation of the realities. If the examples are so numerous that they seem overwhelming and to 'merge into each other', just isolate two or three of them and be as specific as possible.

06. b.   Have I, at any time, indulged in my substance or process of choice more than I intended to? Have I overstepped my own limits?

Think of particular occasions. Give two or three examples. Be as specific as possible. What happened? What were the consequences?

*The questions in 06. c., below, relate to our **preoccupation** with using.*

06. c.   Have I, at any time, allowed my need for my substance or process of choice to interfere with the proper conduct of my life. Have I missed or been late for important appointments? Have I missed work? Have I ignored or neglected my family? Have I got into financial difficulties? Has my 'using' taken precedence over other, more important commitments?
Give four or five examples.
Our using becomes progressively more important to us than anything else. We may not admit this – but our actions show it. In your answers, resist the temptation to generalise. Make them as detailed, as specific and as exact as possible. Avoid, too, the temptation to 'glamorise' or 'humorise' your examples – the attempt to make them seem more acceptable by presenting them to yourself in a humorous or glamorous light.

*The two questions below (06 d. and 06. e.) relate to the **selfishness and irresponsibility** which result from addiction.*

06. d.   Has my using put me or other people in danger, either directly or indirectly? Has it led to road traffic accidents or 'near misses'? Have I put my children at risk? Have I caused accidents at home or at work? Have I been injured? Have other people been injured? *Who? What? When? Where? Give three or four examples.*

06. e.   *Have my work or other responsibilities been adversely affected by my addiction?*
How? When? What was the result? Give several examples.

*Questions 06. f. and 06. g., below, relate to the gradual **erosion of our values** by the progression of addictive disease.*

06. f.   *Have my relationships with loved ones and others been damaged by my behaviour when using?* *Who? How? What happened?*

06. g.   *Have I done things in my addiction of which I ashamed - which are contrary to my own beliefs and principles?* *Give four or five* examples.

When we first begin this process of self-examination, the screen is usually up. We find it difficult and distasteful to identify specific occasions when these things have happened. But gradually we begin to see through the mental screen – and, as time goes by, we remember more and more occasions when our using behaviour has had disastrous consequences for us and for other people. This is a painful process and we shrink from it. Sometimes our 'denial' is so strong that we need others to point out the realities of our predicament. But it is an essential process if we are to begin to get a proper perspective on what has been happening to us and around us – on our complete loss of control over our own lives and the consequences which this has inflicted on others.

*As you begin to remember the details of the havoc which has been occurring in your life, discuss them with your sponsor or with your fellows at meetings in the anonymous fellowships. If this process has helped you to see that you have been powerless to master your addiction – and that your life is consequently unmanageable **by you** – congratulations! You have taken Step One! You are on the first rung of the ladder which will lead you to freedom.*

*Look carefully at the broad picture which is emerging from your answers to the foregoing questions and ask yourself this additional question: **Are these the actions of a sane individual?** As we continue with our work on personal change, we will do well to bear in mind the lessons learned here. There is a temptation, once we are feeling* *healthier, physically and mentally, to forget the misery of active addiction. "What was all the fuss about?" we think " It wasn't really all that bad".*

*It **was** that bad.*

7.   REDISCOVERING TRUST – STEP TWO

It would seem that we are faced with an enormous, almost insoluble, problem. The evidence seems to suggest that we have an incurable illness whose progress we cannot personally arrest – any more than Canute could arrest the progress of the incoming tide. We have only to look honestly at our numerous failed attempts to halt our addictive processes (some of which we noted in Actions 06. a.), to see that this is true. Sometimes we console ourselves with the idea that, next time, it will be different: that, somehow, on our next attempt, we will find the *will-power* to stop. In most cases this is simple self-delusion. The progress of addictive disease can no more be halted by will-power than can the progress of cancer or cystic fibrosis.

This is not to say that alcoholics and addicts of various kinds *lack* will-power – although this is a common misconception among the uninformed. In every other area of our lives, we often display exceptional will-power. Consider the sheer will-power which is required by anorexics in order to starve themselves. Consider the sheer will-power demanded to secure a steady supply of alcohol or other drugs. Consider the prodigious feats which are sometimes required to maintain an addiction. I have known alcoholics living in remote places who would walk ten or fifteen miles in freezing gale-force winds, in the early hours of the morning, for a bottle of whisky. Sir Winston Churchill was almost certainly alcoholic – but few would dare to claim that he lacked will-power. It is simply that *will-power* is not an appropriate faculty to deploy - either against the inexorable tides of the sea or against the advance of an addictive illness.

In many 12-Step treatment centres, patients are introduced to the allegory of the 'sleeping tiger'. Imagine that you have within you a little tiger-cub. This represents your illness in its early phases. In order to remain active your tiger-cub needs a constant supply of your substance or process of choice. When the supply is cut off, it falls asleep. *But it continues to grow.* This means that, if you become abstinent and remain abstinent, even for a number of years, as soon as you recommence your addiction of choice (with a single drink, a single snort or other addictive behaviour) your tiger wakes up. But it is no longer a relatively harmless little cub. It is a gigantic ravening beast.

This, of course, is only a metaphor. But it seems to me to encapsulate some salient truths about addictive disease. Since the release of the series of 'Alien' films, we might like to substitute the image of a tenacious and ferocious alien within. The important point is this. The metaphor suggests that addictive disease continues to progress within us *whether we are actively 'using' or not.* As long as we are abstinent, it does not give us much trouble. But woe betide those who reawaken it. Unhappily, in my own clinical experience, I have known people who have remained abstinent for long periods of time and have then 'reawakened their sleeping tiger'. Some have died within a short space of time. Others, fortunately, have been able to limit the damage, before it was too late.

Let us return to the fundamental dilemma. We saw, in the preceding chapter, that a process which we were powerless to halt had taken control of our lives – and we admitted that, as a result, our lives had become completely unmanageable. In active addiction, it is as though a malevolent force has us in its grip and, struggle as we might, we cannot break free. The power of this malign force seems greater than our own unaided power. A power greater than ourselves appears to be controlling us. What is the solution? The Second Step of the recovery programme gives us the answer.

This is **Step Two:**

We came to believe that a power greater than ourselves could restore us to sanity.

It is reasonable to suppose that, in order to counteract the destructive effects of a malignant power that is greater than us, we shall need a countervailing and benign force which is even more powerful. That this powerful countervailing force exists is now a matter of record. The restored sanity and renewed lives of millions throughout the world attest to the fact. What is the nature of this healing power?

For our present purposes the answer is very simple. Every day, we see examples where group action achieves a result which individual action is incapable of encompassing. Let us imagine that we wish to send a manned spacecraft to Venus. Is it reasonable to go out into our back garden and begin assembling the craft on our own? No. We assemble a *team* of the greatest experts we can find who are *dedicated to the same end.* The greatest experts in the field of addiction, in all of its various manifestations, are not necessarily the professionals: the doctors, the therapists, the learned professors, the consultant psychiatrists sporting bow-ties, the psychologists - nor even the counsellors like myself. It must be frankly admitted that the record of medicine, and of psychiatry in particular, in producing whole, happy, healed individuals who have recovered from this illness, is rather poor. The greatest experts in this field are the addicts and alcoholics themselves. Add to this a purposeful dedication to the cause of recovery and you have an unbeatable team. Add to this a research programme which has already produced a blueprint and a wealth of experience – a programme of recovery which has been shown to work more than a million times over - and you have an insuperable team.

Luckily for all of us these teams already exist all over the world in the form of the anonymous fellowships. And provided you are an expert in the field, an addict of some kind, and are dedicated to the goal of your own personal recovery, they are happy to welcome you into the team free of charge.

One of the implications of Step Two is that we are actually insane. If we need to be restored to sanity by a power greater than ourselves then, presumably, we must be insane. Newcomers often have some difficulty in accepting this proposition.

I have mentioned that, prior to becoming acquainted with this recovery programme, I often used to find myself in psychiatric hospitals of various kinds. Usually, in the general psychiatric wards of these hospitals, there was a handful of other addicts and alcoholics who were also undergoing detoxification. It did not take us long to identify each other. But there were also many other patients who had been hospitalised for a wide range of other psychiatric disorders – bipolar disease (manic depressive illness), schizophrenia, etc., etc. Invariably the little group of addicts and alcoholics would gravitate towards each other and sit separately from the other 'loonies'. We, after all, were not *real* loonies. We had just 'over-indulged' a bit and had got a bit wrecked. And yet now, looking back on it all, I can see very clearly that some of our actions while we were out there in the world, drinking and using, were a great deal more 'insane' than anything that had been done by the other 'psychiatric' cases. By any objective standard our own behaviour had been utterly insane. We had destroyed spouses, families and property. Sometimes, either intentionally or unintentionally, we had taken other people's lives. We had sabotaged jobs, crippled businesses and flouted the law. Our actions may have been violent and criminal. At the very least we may have pestered others with long, incoherent, tearful telephone conversations. We had wreaked havoc upon other people and upon the world. Is that not insane? I can see now that it was *we* who were the real 'loonies'.

As we shall see later, it is unfortunately true that, when we stop using, all this insanity does not immediately disappear. We are still insane. I am still insane. However, we can keep our insanity at bay *by working this programme on a daily basis.*

The observant reader will have noticed that this chapter on Step Two was entitled **Rediscovering Trust**. For some of us it may be more a case of discovering trust for the first time. Usually during our lives in active addiction we have trusted nothing but ourselves and our substance or process of choice. As it turns out, that trust has been misplaced. Our own judgment has been found wanting. Our substances and processes have proved treacherous. But how can we possibly trust a power greater than ourselves?

We have provisionally defined that 'power' as a programme of recovery and a team of people like ourselves. We have seen, in meetings of the anonymous fellowships, countless people who have been restored to sanity by these means. A power greater than themselves appears to have accomplished this *for them*. Is it possible that it might also work for *us*? We have nothing to lose from trying it. Often, in the fellowships, you will hear the expression 'Fake it to make it'. Even if we have not yet 'come to believe' *fully* that this programme can work for us, let us behave as though it will. Coming to believe may be a process. It does not have to be an event.

ACTIONS   *07.*

For those who are not able to go for 'treatment', it may be of interest to know that in many 12-Step treatment centres patients are sometimes asked to participate in 'Trust Games'. These are often also used in drama-training and in team-building for businesses. The aim is to develop the ability to trust your peers. Some are comparatively simple. An individual is blindfolded and allows himself or herself to be led around by a guide in an environment where there are obstacles of various kinds. Usually the 'guide' will give a quiet and comprehensive commentary, consisting of a description of the obstacles and suggestions as to how they may be negotiated. The 'subject', wearing the blindfold, is obliged to entrust himself or herself entirely to the care of the guide. If the exercise is properly conducted, no mishaps will befall either the guide, who is not blindfolded, or the subject, who is.

A variation on this game places the blindfolded subject upright in the centre of a standing circle of their peers. The subject is instructed to allow him/her-self to 'fall' backwards or forwards or sideways. It is the job of the surrounding group to 'catch' the subject, so that no injuries are sustained. The surrounding group may be placed closely around the subject or further away, to allow a greater 'falling distance'. Group members take it in turn to be the 'subject'.

There are direct analogies in these two games between the position of the individual who is blindfolded and the position of the newcomer to the anonymous fellowships. We must allow ourselves to be guided and supported.

*If you are undertaking recovery without the benefit of a readily available group, you may find it difficult to arrange to participate in trust-building exercises of this sort. But there are a number of simple things which you **can** do:*

07. a.   *Write a letter.*

Address it correctly. Stick an appropriate stamp on it. Post it.

After three or four days check whether it has arrived at its destination.

*Repeat this exercise ten or twenty times. Record the number of times that your letters do reach their destinations – and the number of times that they don't. From this information, calculate the statistical probability that your letters will reach their intended destinations. From this we learn that, by and large, we **can** trust the postal services. The postal services are perhaps not necessarily a power **greater** than ourselves. But they are certainly a power **outside** of ourselves. On the whole, we can depend upon **others** to do what they say they will do.*

We may also draw the conclusion that, if we perform the appropriate actions in the right order, we shall obtain a reasonably predictable result.

07. b.   *Turn on an electric light switch.*

Repeat this action at random intervals over a ten- or twenty-day period. Record the number of times the light comes on and the number of times it doesn't. Draw your own conclusions about the dependability of the electricity company and whether or not electricity is a power greater than you

07. c. **Make a list of things which you consider to be powers 'greater than yourself'.**

This might include some of the stupendous forces of nature – or it might include social organisations, such as the police force. The test is whether you can control it or not. If you can't, it is (at least in some senses) greater than you.

07. d. **Go to your favourite meeting of one of the Anonymous Fellowships.**

Talk to two or three of the people there whom you consider to be most 'well'.
*Ask them what they **did** to get well.*

Do you believe that you can do the same things? Do you believe that you, too, can get well?

If you do – congratulations! You have taken Step Two.

8. RELINQUISHING THE REINS – STEP THREE

"Help! It's the God Squad!" I thought, when I first encountered Step Three.

I am not going to argue about semantics. Ultimately, it seems to me that the whole argument about the existence or otherwise of some kind of God boils down to a question of semantics. It depends, in other words, on what you mean by the word 'God'. Let me tell you a true story to illustrate this point. At the age of fifteen, like most teenagers, I was an omniscient sage. I was also a rabid, proselytising, missionary atheist.

At my school we were obliged to attend compulsory Chapel every day – and twice on Sundays. I was waging a campaign to have this custom discontinued – to make Chapel voluntary (I still think this would have been a good idea). For the Religious Education classes, which they called 'Divinity' and which were also compulsory (unless you happened to be a Muslim, a Hindu, a Sikh, a Jew or a Catholic), I had nothing but contempt. On my weekly timetable, in the box where 'Divinity' should have appeared, I had written 'Magic' dismissively. The 'holy beaks', masters who were also ordained Anglican priests, were objects of my derision. So virulent had I become in my opposition to all religion that my school decided to send me to attend a five-day conference.

The conference, which had been given some ghastly, snappy theme like 'Facing Up To God', was held in a monastery in Oxford, belonging to the Society of St John the Evangelist – the 'Cowley Fathers', an Anglican monastic order. There were, perhaps, twenty other boys attending the conference from schools across the UK. Each day, we were split up into 'discussion groups' of five or six and invited to discuss some 'relevant' topic. In the afternoon, each group presented its conclusions and a general discussion ensued, under the chairmanship of the Father Superior - who was at that time, I believe, called Fr Campbell.

By the end of the second day, it had already emerged that I considered myself an atheist. I had ambitions to convert all the other boys to atheism.

"Ah, that's very interesting, John" said Fr Campbell, just before tea "So… You're an atheist, then?"

"Of course I am." said I "I don't know how any intelligent, modern human being could possibly believe in all these primitive fairy-stories about a God."

"Oh, dear." said old Fr Campbell "You don't believe in God, then?"

"Of course not," I declared "It's all foolish old-wives tales."

"Aah!" drawled Fr Campbell in his funny shaky old voice, looking down at his thumbs. Then he raised his head and looked me straight in the eyes. "Tell me, John," he said softly "*which* God is it that you don't believe in?"

I was a little discomposed by his question and by his piercing eyes – and muttered something about not believing in any God. But by the following morning I had recovered my wits and was launched with renewed vigour on my mission to sew corrupting doubts in the minds of my innocent contemporaries. It was not until many years later that I began to realise the significance of Fr Campbell's question. With the benefit of hindsight, I can see that the only God I did not believe in was a God which I had constructed in my own mind from scraps of religious material – 'Divinity' lessons, the bible, a superficial knowledge of other world faiths, ecclesiastical ceremonies, tedious sermons and improbable stories about 'loaves and fishes' etc., etc. And I had constructed this idea of 'God' with a single purpose in mind: to make it as unbelievable and as ridiculous as possible. But might there not be another God? A God about whom I knew little or nothing. A God, perhaps, that was far beyond my own, poor, limited human understanding.

It is for these reasons that I now consider atheism a technical impossibility. If I say "I do not believe in God", all I am actually saying is that I do not believe in my own concept of God. It is, in other words, a confession of the inadequacy of my own imagination. All I am actually saying is "I cannot conceive of a God in which I could believe." And, no matter how elegantly the thought may be dressed up, this, in the end, is all that is being said by people like the distinguished Professor Richard Dawkins and many other old-fashioned, militant, antitheistic zealots. Dawkins confuses two quite separate issues. From the fact that much of what is called 'religion' is plainly tripe, it does not and cannot follow that there is no God. There is no more evidence to demonstrate that there is no God than there is to show that there is one. Atheism, in this sense, is just a primitive superstition popularised by the intellectual vogues of the 1950s and 1960s.

Similarly, the fact that some people appear to have an emotional need for God (the old 'crutch' argument) cannot in any way imply that there is no God. Fortunately for those who have skiing accidents, crutches *do* exist. We all *need* (for instance) oxygen. Luckily for us, oxygen exists. Indeed, it might with equal justice be argued that human beings are not generally equipped with needs for which there is no corresponding satisfaction. On this reckoning, the need of humankind for some sort of a Divinity may be said, if anything, to militate rather in favour of the existence of such a Being.

Step Three reads as follows:

We made a decision to turn our will and our lives over to the care of God *as we understood Him.*

This is **not**, therefore, the God of any particular religion. It is a God of our own understanding. It may be that our own concept of God *does* coincide to a large extent with the understanding of God presented by one of the great religions of the world. It may be that it doesn't. Our own concept of God may be distinctly idiosyncratic. It doesn't matter. The Anonymous Fellowships are not religious and are not cults. Unlike religions and cults, there is no *doctrine* which must be believed by members. There are Hindus, Buddhists, Jews, Christians, Muslims and Zoroastrians in the fellowships. There are adherents of Wicca, of Taoism, Animism and of every kind of belief-system and philosophy. There are even a few Satanists and Chartered Accountants. The fellowships, surprisingly, are full of atheists and agnostics. Many feel no need for a God of any kind and are happy to continue to regard the Fellowship itself as a Higher Power. I have heard of a member who, back in the Seventies (when such things were not unknown) chose a giant octopus called Boris as his Higher Power. It seemed to work for him – and nobody tried to alter his beliefs. Many hold that God works principally through the words and actions of other people.

"There are only two things you need to know about the Higher Power" my first sponsor used to say: "There is one – and you're not it."

If we elect ourselves, or our own 'inner wisdom', as our Higher Power, we are heading for trouble. All too often, you will hear trendy 'therapists' and 'counsellors' urging people to 'trust your instincts' or to 'follow your heart'. This is the worst possible advice which can be given to any recovering addict or alcoholic. The *last* thing that anyone suffering from an addictive disorder can afford to be guided by is the 'intuition' of their own heart or mind. After a long career of active addiction, it is unlikely that we shall have much 'inner wisdom'. Most of us, indeed, have acted on our 'intuitions' for most of our lives – usually with disastrous consequences. So what *are* we to do?

Let's look again at **Step Three**. The first thing we note is that it requires a *decision*. As I have said before, this is not a theoretical programme. It is an intensely *practical* programme of recovery. It does not point us towards an endless speculative debate. It impels us through a succession of *actions and decisions*. A decision is not a decision unless it is accompanied by a change in attitude or behaviour. Without these, it is merely an intention. A decision, moreover, is irrevocable. We may, indeed, make a subsequent decision which modifies our original decision – but, by that time, the effects of our original decision will already have been felt. What, exactly, is it that we are deciding to do in Step Three? We have decided to 'turn our will and our lives over' to the 'care' of a Higher Power. How, precisely, do we do this?

My sponsor once said to me "Listen, John. If you want to bake a nice cake – and you've never done it before - how are you going to set about it?" I immediately launched into a complicated rigmarole about flour and baking powder, cooking times and oven temperatures, eggs, rising time and raisins. With difficulty, he managed to stop me in mid-flow. "No, no, no, no, *no,*" he said "YOU FOLLOW THE RECIPE !"

In this context, then, turning our will and our lives over to the care of a higher power means, quite simply, making a decision to follow the recipe. Not our own recipe – but **the** recipe – the 12 Step recovery programme. To many people with an addictive personality, this is anathema. We tend to be extreme individualists. The idea of 'toeing the party line' is repugnant to us. But it is important to note three things in this context.

First of all, it is *our own* decision. Nobody decides for us. First, last and always *we* make the decision.

Secondly, we are not *handing over* our will and our lives to anything or anybody. We are *turning* them over. Each day of our lives is replete with challenges and problems of one kind or another. Unfortunately, this Step is often misquoted and misunderstood by well-meaning counsellors who exhort their clients to 'hand over' their problems to their higher power. "Hand it over", I have heard them say. To me this seems like an abdication of responsibility. The programme mentions nothing whatsoever about 'handing it over' to a higher power or to anything else. We cannot simply forget about our problems. We need instead to continue to seek the solutions to these problems – *but under the guidance of a higher power*. For all practical purposes, this usually means under the guidance of our sponsor and of our friends in the Fellowship. There are occasions, too, when the solution to a particular problem is neither what we expect, nor, perhaps, what we had hoped for. We cannot always impose our own solutions on particular problems. Nor can we always impose our own time-frame. This is especially the case when other people are involved in the nature of the problem. At such times, we simply have to play our own part, to the best of our ability, and leave the outcome to a wisdom that is greater than our own. The solution which eventually emerges is usually better than anything we ourselves could have devised.

Thirdly, therefore, we should note that we are turning our will and our lives over to the *care* of a higher power. We are not renouncing our autonomy. We are simply entrusting our proper use of that autonomy to a power greater than ourselves. In view of the *improper* use which we have all too often made of our autonomy in the past, this would seem to be quite a sensible thing to do.

ACTIONS   *08.*

Before performing these Actions, you need to ask yourself a question. Are you prepared to go to almost any lengths in order to get well and stay well? Before answering this question, spend a little time considering the extraordinary lengths to which you used to go in order to sustain your addiction and gradually destroy yourself. Are you prepared to go to similar lengths for the sake of your health, wholeness and happiness?

You are now going to start taking more responsibility for your own recovery.

08. a.   **Get hold of a copy of the AA 'Big Book' – Alcoholics Anonymous.**
How you do this is up to you.

08. b.   *Take it to your Sponsor and turn to page 63. Read through the prayer, half way down the page. If you wish, paraphrase it into a form with which you feel comfortable. You might, for instance, want to replace all the 'thees' and 'thous' with more modern pronouns.*

08. c.   *Preferably with your sponsor, get down on your knees (or assume any other posture which may be appropriate to your beliefs).*
Say the prayer together.

It doesn't matter if you don't know to whom or to what you are praying. It doesn't matter if you feel foolish. Just do it.

In one sense, this is an unique and special moment for you. You have just taken Step Three. Many people, however, find that it is useful to remember this prayer and to renew this commitment in a quiet moment every morning

9.   REALISM – STEP FOUR

In Step Four we begin to free ourselves of some of our deeply embedded, long-term resentments. A surprising number of people, when they first encounter Step Four, say, in all seriousness, "That won't be a problem. I haven't got any resentments." And they really believe this to be true. But we cannot be rid of our resentments unless we are first able to acknowledge them, however trivial they may seem.

Equally, there are many people who may have suffered terrible physical, mental, emotional or sexual abuse and who are understandably filled with rage and bitterness – but who shy away from dealing directly with the causes of their anguish. The memories are just too painful. We would prefer to keep them buried in oblivion, never to be revealed to anyone. On no account do we wish them to be brought into the open.

There are also some who believe that these or other traumatic experiences (abandonment, rejection, bereavement, etc.) have *caused* them to become addicts.

As we shall see, none of these attitudes or beliefs are particularly helpful to recovery. The main reason for freeing ourselves from the poison of resentment is that, if we do not, these destructive feelings can propel us into a state of relapse.

At my school, nearly forty years ago, any small boy who was half-presentable got beaten and buggered by older boys – and sometimes by masters. I don't know whether they still maintain these quaint customs but, in those days, it was pretty routine. I, at any rate, did not manage to escape this fate.

There. I said it. It was not so difficult. Yet this was one of the 'deep, dark secrets' which I lugged around with me till the age of thirty seven. It was one of the reasons why, at the age of sixteen, I decided to scarper from school.

One fine spring morning, in 1967, as the sun was beginning to lift the ephemeral wisps of mist which adorned the playing-fields and meadows, I set out with a contemporary companion, on a journey that would take us to Marseille, Aix-en-Provence and freedom. It did not take us long to run out of money and, eventually, we had to be repatriated by the British Consul in Marseille. But that is another story.

I mention it here for a number of reasons, which I hope will become apparent.

Step Four reads as follows:

We made a searching and fearless moral inventory of ourselves.

In many 12-Step treatment centres, **Step Four** is turned into a Very Big Deal Indeed. Patients who are 'on Step Four' wander around the treatment centre looking hollow-eyed, dazed and anxious. But I do not believe that it needs to be a VBDI. It is true that, in Step Four, we shall be taking our 'examination of conscience', begun in **Step One**, to a deeper level. It is likely, therefore, that we shall experience a similar discomfort and reluctance to face the realities of our addiction and of our entire lives.

In treatment centres, much emphasis is usually placed upon 'feeling the feelings' associated with people and events from our past. By the time we start on the road to recovery, most of us have a mountainous 'emotional backlog' – the tangled and accumulated mass of feelings which we have tried to suppress or abolish by 'using'.

In order to become healthy we need to resolve these feelings. But this is **not** the main purpose of Step Four.

The originators of this programme describe Step Four in a rather different way. They describe it as 'making an inventory'. When shopkeepers or householders make their inventory, they do not usually linger on each item to 'feel the feelings' associated with that item. The resolution of emotional conflicts *is* a necessary process, if we want to get well and stay well. But Step Four is not necessarily the right place to seek this therapeutic benefit. We have eight more Steps – and the rest of our lives – to address our 'issues'. At this early point in our recovery, we need to get on with our programme of actions and decisions. It is, I believe, for this reason that the pioneers of recovery recommend a very simple approach to Step Four. They recommend, firstly, that our inventory should be 'searching and fearless'. Secondly they make clear that we are making a moral inventory *of ourselves* – not of our enemies, not of our parents, not of our teachers, not of our employers, not of our spouses or families – just ourselves. Thirdly, they suggest that, rather than trying to feel *all* of our different feelings, we should concentrate on **one** feeling in particular – resentment.

We shall return, in a moment, to the whip-wielding pederasts of my school some forty years ago – or, rather, to my own *reactions* to these experiences. But first, it might be as well to review, briefly, what we have already done. At the very least, this is what we have accomplished so far:

We have admitted *and continue to admit* that we are powerless over our addictive illness – and that our lives are consequently unmanageable by us.

We think it at any rate possible that a power greater than ourselves can restore us to some semblance of sanity.

We have made a decision that, this day and every day, we shall allow ourselves to be guided by a wisdom that is greater than our own.

If we *have* done these things, we have already accomplished something which, for an addict of any description, is quite stupendous. Most of us, in our lives hitherto, have been wilful in the extreme. We have been unwilling to concede that there might even *be* any wisdom greater than our own. We have insisted upon remaining in the driving seat. We have ignored and dismissed the concerns and advice of others. We have repeatedly driven the vehicle of our own destinies into various brick-walls, often with hostages on board. One way or another (and without necessarily intending to) we have smashed and wrecked our lives and the lives of many around us. It is extremely difficult and unnatural for us to learn new habits – but we are gradually getting there.

At the end of Chapter 6., we congratulated ourselves on having mounted the first rung of a ladder that would lead us to freedom. There is another metaphor which is, perhaps, more apposite. It is as though we are erecting a staircase from solid building blocks. Our foundation is Step One. Upon this foundation we build Step Two. We add Step Three. And so on upwards. For this recovery programme is not so much sequential as *cumulative*. We cannot simply 'do' Step One – and then forget about it. We have to ensure that our 'foundation' remains in place. If Step One (or any of the Steps) crumbles away, the whole superstructure will probably tumble down. If I lose sight of the fact that I am powerless over my addictive disorder, I might be tempted to step back into the boxing-ring with it - to try another round or two. It will pulverise me, of course, just as it always has done in the past. The reason that, nowadays, I choose on a daily basis not to use alcohol or other mood-altering drugs is **not** that I have somehow 'conquered' them. Quite the opposite. It is simply the hard-won knowledge that, if I do step into the ring with them, they will annihilate me. And, where my addiction is concerned, I have learned to be a devout coward.

Back to the quaint customs at schools like mine in the 1960s. I will not join that bluff and hearty chorus, whose doughty chant is "It did us no harm!". I believe that, for the most part, those who make this claim are whistling in the dark - to keep their spirits up. It seems to me that being buggered and flogged with cane and birch, in early adolescence, can do untold psychological damage. Well into the latter half of the twentieth century, such schools served as the seminaries of sado-masochism. Certainly, in my own case, it left me somewhat confused about my own sexual identity throughout my teens. It was not until I reached my twenties that I realised that I was enthusiastically heterosexual. But, oddly enough, in the context of Step Four, none of this is particularly pertinent - *unless* such experiences leave us embittered and with long-term **resentments**.

What *is* pertinent, therefore, is that, as a result of all this, I certainly *was* left with one or two minor resentments. This, to put it plainly, is an understatement. For many years I regarded these school experiences as one of the *causes* of my addiction. It was very convenient for me to blame my addiction on traumatic experiences in my youth – and to blame my parents for letting me go to that particular school. In fact, of course, like most parents, they were simply doing the best they could with the information at their disposal. But I still remember the dreadful impotent rage I felt, at the age of fifteen, after being severely caned, in a particularly humiliating way, by my House Captain (a 19 year old), not for any specific offence - but for "general slackness"!

What this actually meant was that they disapproved of my long hair and suspected me of smoking cigarettes – and enjoyed laying stripes upon the bottoms of young boys.

To the Headmaster alone belonged the right of chastising boys' *naked* buttocks with a specially constructed bundle of supple birch sprigs. It was a right of which he availed himself whenever the opportunity arose, while masturbating furiously in his trouser pocket – as I have good reason to know. He had been in a Japanese prisoner-of-war camp, poor man. He was very sick.

For years, I plotted dire, dramatic and bloodthirsty revenge scenes for the floggings which I received at school. Luckily, they remained imaginary.

I now believe that, although these and other similar experiences may well have *triggered* my active addiction, they did not *cause* my underlying addictive disease. I was almost certainly born with that. I had started getting drunk, whenever I had access to alcohol, *before* all these things happened. The year before I absconded from my school, I had already been 'busted' by the school authorities for smoking cannabis (I had been trying to emulate De Quincey and Coleridge, Huxley and Burroughs, Leary, Ginsberg, Kerouac and the rest).

Besides, other people get beaten and buggered - but, somehow, they manage to deal with the emotional consequences without resorting to addiction of one kind or another. They do not feel *compelled* to resort to mood-altering substances or processes. The born addict, on the other hand, can find no other way to handle distress (or any other feeling). Nevertheless, I am perfectly certain that the resentments occasioned by these experiences *kept* me sick for a very long time. And so did my secrets. For I never spoke of any of this until I entered 'treatment', for the first time, in my thirty eighth year.

"You're as sick as your secrets" runs one of the axioms often heard in the meeting-rooms of the various fellowships. I do not pretend to understand fully *why* our unshared 'baggage' keeps us sick. I am pretty sure that it is related to unacknowledged feelings of fear, guilt and shame. We 'use' on our feelings. Nor do I pretend to understand fully the psychological mechanism which heals us. For some reason, when we speak those things which we have previously regarded as unspeakable, we get well. When we bring into the light those things which we have diligently cloaked in darkness, they lose their power over us. When we find that others can accept, in a non-judgmental way, those events and characteristics which we have been unable to accept in ourselves, it helps us to come to terms with them – and to move on.

I never wanted to disclose the events with which this chapter began to anyone. I was fully resolved to take these 'secrets' with me to the grave. I remember well the trepidation with which I approached a mini-group (composed of peers whom I felt I could trust and selected by me for the purpose), when I realised, during my first treatment, that I would have to 'speak the unspeakable'. In my mind, I had turned this process of disclosure into a Very Big Deal Indeed. After I had poured it all out in a halting and tremulous voice, there was a brief silence. Then one of the girls in the group said:

"Oh. Is that all ?"

She then proceeded to tell us about comparable episodes in her own life. Others in the group, including the males, contributed their own similar feelings and experiences. By the end of the group, we were all laughing – not at the tragic and distressing events themselves, but at our own fierce determination never to reveal such things to anyone. In reality, this process of 'opening up' had proved to be No Big Deal!

Statistically, it is probably true that there is a higher incidence of sexual, physical and emotional abuse in childhood among addicts and alcoholics who come into treatment than might be expected in a typical cross-section of the community as a whole. But it would be facile to imagine that there must therefore be some causal connection between early abuse and later addictive behaviours. The two may indeed go together - but this does not show that abuse *causes* addiction. An individual whose family background includes alcoholism or addiction may well be more likely to have been exposed to abuse. These individuals, however, would also *inherit* the genetic predisposition to addiction. Similarly, although the levels of abuse reported by people who come into treatment for addictive disorders may appear to be higher than those of the general population, this phenomenon may well be related to the levels of reporting. Other victims of abuse, who do not have addictive disease, and who adapt to its consequences in other ways, are not so likely to end up in some form of treatment where such matters come to light. Nevertheless, abuse in some form (and at any stage of life) may well be one of the factors which trigger latent addictive disease into active addiction.

Nor are these the only kinds of secret which keep us sick. The darkest secrets, the ones which we hang on to most tenaciously, are more often to do with the ways in which we have abused or harmed others. These are the ones which require real courage to face and to own. It is a truism that those who have been abused often become abusers themselves. Here, more than anywhere, is where we need to be searching and thorough.

Although much of the anxiety associated with embarking upon Steps 4 and 5 is often linked to a disinclination to examine our sexual behaviours and 'hang-ups', this aspect of our lives is only *one* of the many sets of behaviours we shall look at. It cannot be stressed enough that these two Steps are **not** to be regarded as a 'confession' of our 'sins'. The intention is not to give us an overwhelming sense of our own moral turpitude. At some unarticulated level, we probably have that already – in an exaggerated form. Disproportionate feelings of guilt and shame have often kept us 'using'.

The intention here is simply to bring to light some of the issues which are impeding our progress – and to **begin** to deal with them in a constructive and healing way. How can this be done?

ACTIONS   *09.*

*At present, we do not need to worry about when, or how, or to whom we are going to disclose those events in our lives of which we are not particularly proud. We are 'disclosing' them only to ourselves. We know that, in Step Five, we shall make such admissions to at least one other human being. But here, in **Step Four**, we are simply going to acknowledge these matters to ourselves and to examine what their emotional consequences have been – for us.*

I have seen many different types of Fourth Step worksheet in use in various treatment centres. Most of them seem to me to over-complicate the matter. They have a tendency to turn Step Four into a Bigger Deal than it needs to be. Let us, therefore, try to stick as closely as possible to the intentions of those who originated this programme. Let's keep it simple.

*Certainly, we need to be as thorough as possible – but we also need to guard against perfectionism. A wise friend once said to me "If you want perfection or nothing, you'll always get nothing." You will often hear it said in the Fellowships that we aim for **progress** – not perfection.*

There is a very simple schema in the AA 'Big Book' to help us with Step Four. I have found it to be more useful, on the whole, than all the complicated worksheets devised by the various treatment centres.

*The originators of this programme advise us to look back over our lives – starting from the present day – and to list all of the people and institutions against whom we are **still** harbouring **resentments**. We do not have to do this in a **precisely** reverse chronological order. All we need to do, for the present, is to get down on paper our **main** resentments: the really big ones. Oddly enough, the intensity of our resentments against people or institutions may bear little relation to the magnitude of the apparent cause. I felt a far greater resentment towards a former friend who had deliberately ignored or 'cut' me at a debutante's ball than I did towards the mugger who robbed me and broke my nose in an Underground station when I was drunk. I felt a far greater resentment against the firm of wine merchants who had me* *arrested (for attempting to steal an enormous bottle of vintage port) than I did against the magistrate who fined me £150 – a huge sum for me in 1985!*

*Next to the person or institution against whom we are harbouring a resentment, let us, therefore, list the **cause** (real or imaginary) of our resentful feelings.*

*And finally, let us consider **why**, precisely, these circumstances have given rise to such intense feelings of resentment within us. We shall find, usually, that it is because they have hit us at an intensely personal level. When Ian B. deliberately chose to ignore me when I spoke to him at that ball back in 1969, I felt humiliated. He had not only ignored me – it seemed to me that he had made a point of ignoring me **in public**. I felt crushed and annihilated.*

For various reasons I do not like the term 'self-esteem' – but it is a convenient shorthand term. It would be no exaggeration to say that being 'cut' at a ball – in the presence of so many of my friends and acquaintances – dented my 'self-esteem' somewhat! In a later chapter, we shall be examining the reasons for this.

For now, however, it is enough simply to note that it did. Using the examples which I have given above - and one or two others - let's see what our Step Four schema is beginning to look like. At this point, you might like to begin your own grid on several sheets of A4 paper.

Against whom do I harbour resentments?	Why? What happened?	How did (does) this affect me personally?
Amelia	Wouldn't have sex with me. She doesn't find me attractive.	Gives me a low opinion of myself. Not good for my self-esteem. Felt sexually insecure.
Messrs **Bottoms Up** – Wine Merchants of Haywards Heath	They had me arrested for attempting to steal their port.	Having this on my record makes me look bad. Not good for my self-esteem. Affected my employment prospects and financial security. Felt fearful.
Haywards Heath magistrates.	Fined me £150	Ditto (as above) Hit me financially at the time. Felt insecure and fearful.
Ian B.	Publicly 'cut' me at the deb's ball. Made me look foolish.	Might have given others a low opinion of me. They may have laughed at me. Not good for my self-esteem. Felt fearful and insecure.
Headmaster at school.	Flogged me for smoking dope. Masturbated while doing it.	Painful. I felt degraded and humiliated. Not good for my self-esteem. Felt stupid for getting caught. Anger. Fear.
Etc.	Etc.	Etc.

*In considering our schema, as it develops, we can see that it has a number of interesting features. The first thing which is apparent is that many of the resentments, illogically, are against people or institutions **whom we have harmed**. Messrs Bottoms Up certainly did not deserve to have their port stolen. All they did was to uphold their rights. Why should I feel resentful about that?*

The answer, of course, is in the third column – and it is to this column that we should pay particular attention. Even on those occasions when it may be argued, justifiably, that we ourselves were not at fault, there is often nevertheless a selfish aspect to our feelings of resentment. We may have been affected financially or in terms of our self-esteem or personal security. Our own comfort or convenience may have been disturbed. Perhaps we have not managed to get something which we wanted. Perhaps we have not been able to get our own way over some issue. At the root of it all, underlying all of our resentments, is the sense that something has happened which was not in our own personal interests. This, in turn, can give rise to intense feelings of anger arising from fear and insecurity. There is nothing particularly 'abnormal' about this. But we need to resolve these feelings if we wish to get well.

*During the course of anybody's life, however, there **are** some incidents which, quite simply, are not our fault. They are mercifully rare. For the most part, we are the architects of our own misfortunes. We ourselves play some part in bringing about the situations which perturb us.*

*But even when by no stretch of the imagination can we be said to have had any part in an adverse occurrence, we **still** need to free ourselves of the resentments which are engendered. Even when we think our resentments wholly justified, we still need to be rid of them. This can be extremely difficult – but we need to do it **for our own sakes**. If we walk around in the world embittered and with unresolved feelings of resentment, we harm only ourselves. Our adversaries probably sleep easy – while we are burned-up with hatred. Nurturing resentments is not much fun and it prevents us from enjoying our own lives. It is we who suffer. And when we are suffering – through fear, hatred, bitterness or insecurity - we are much more likely to 'use'. It is as simple as that.*

*In the chapters which follow, we shall be looking at some of the ways in which we can free ourselves of even our most deep-seated resentments and at the methods and attitudes which can drive out fear and insecurity. The important point here, in Step Four, is that we have made a very good start. If we have gone back through our lives and have listed, as far as we can presently remember, all the people and organisations against whom we **still** feel resentments, we have already accomplished a great deal. If we have managed to see that many of those resentments are ultimately unjustifiable, we have already begun the process of freeing ourselves. In Step Five, we shall be taking that process further.*

*The authors of the AA Big Book recommend two further additions to our Step Four work. Firstly they suggest that we should assess, on paper (freehand), our sexual behaviours: not in order to find causes and manifestations of our addictions, but simply in order to become aware of instances where we have been selfish, dishonest or inconsiderate towards others. Have other people been hurt or harmed as a result of our actions? Has our behaviour given rise to jealousy, suspicion, bitterness? Because we are addicts, we are very good at justifying to ourselves behaviour which is actually unjustifiable. My pursuit, mentioned earlier, of a married woman (whose husband was a friend of mine) is a case in point. At the time, I found all kinds of spurious reasons for continuing this relationship. ('Their marriage was in trouble anyway, before I came along', 'She didn't know what she was doing when she married him', ' She and I are soul-mates in a way that she never could be with him' etc., etc.) But the truth is that I was just being selfish. My actions, moreover, may well have contributed to the subsequent breakdown of their marriage. He, she and their children were certainly damaged by my behaviour. It took me a long time to be able to recognise this. But in Step Four, we need to be scrupulously honest **with ourselves**.*

Secondly, however, the authors of the AA Big Book suggest that, having noted how many of our resentments have their root in fear of one sort or another, we should actually begin to confront our worst fears directly, by getting them down on paper. Do this in whatever manner suits you best. You can write a comprehensive analysis of your fears – or you can make brief notes. This action alone should help you to get them into a better perspective and should tell you much about the wellsprings of your own actions and reactions. When you come to discuss them with your sponsor (or whoever hears your Step Five) this process will be further advanced.

Finally, no Step Four is complete unless it also takes account of the resentments which we feel **against ourselves**. These can often be the most troublesome. If we are feeling uneasy, guilty or ashamed about certain matters, we may need to do something to redress the situation. We shall be looking more closely at **how** this can be done in Steps Eight and Nine.

"How could I have been so stupid?", "Why on earth did I do that?", "I should have... (done something else)" These are the kind of sentiments which are usually very familiar to those whose lives have been blighted by an addictive illness. Fruitless regrets can be almost as poisonous as resentments against other people. Often, they are simply a form of resentment against ourselves. Usually we have done some senseless thing (or failed to do a sensible thing) for a very simple reason. **We have been extremely sick**. We are probably only just beginning to realise exactly how sick we **have** been. This is good news. It means that we are getting well.

10. TRANSPARENCY - STEP FIVE

In most primary treatment centres, patients are not taken beyond Step Five. I know of at least one treatment centre where all twelve Steps are introduced but, in most, the Fifth Step is usually the last of the twelve Steps which is undertaken while still in primary treatment. Having completed this Step the patient is usually discharged, either back into the community at large, or with a referral to a 'halfway house', for a period of stabilisation and of less intensive 'secondary' treatment. This is sometimes known as 'extended' or 'secondary' care. Sometimes, the patient is advised that their primary treatment has been no more than an intensive introduction to the recovery programme – and that they would do well to recommence the whole process from Step One, in the outside world, under the guidance of a Sponsor from one of the anonymous fellowships. My friend and mentor, Dr Robert Lefever (founder of The PROMIS Recovery Centre), sometimes says that treatment has only one main purpose – to get people suffering from addictive disorders into the anonymous fellowships.

If you have been following these chapters methodically, even without the benefit of residential treatment, the need to start again should not arise. But it may. I myself had to start again several times – because I kept relapsing. A relapse is a pretty good indication that some essential part of the Programme has not been properly digested. Quite apart from anything else, it is usually a pretty good indication that Step One has not been fully absorbed. If we are fully and permanently conscious of our powerlessness over our addictive substances and processes, we avoid them like the plague. We remain abstinent. But if we allow ourselves to listen to the subtle doubts which our disease will try to implant in our minds, we are vulnerable to relapse. If we then decide to conduct some more practical 'research' into the question of whether or not we can afford to 'dabble' with our substances or processes of choice, we shall almost certainly end up back in Gomorrah within a short space of time. This, at any rate, has been my experience. Personally, I feel that I have now done quite enough of this type of research work. The result has always been the same. Nowadays, therefore, I prefer to leave this kind of 'research' to others – and would suggest that you do the same. There is, after all, an extraordinarily high mortality rate in Gomorrah. Some of the people who go back there never get away again. A relapse can be fatal.

Stepping back into the ring with your addictive disease is like stepping into the ring with Mike Tyson. At the very least, you will end up severely damaged.

It is, of course, possible to limit the damage which a relapse inevitably entails. Towards the end of this book, you will find a number of ideas, both about 'relapse prevention' and about what to do in the event of a relapse. I hope that you will never need the latter. For now, however, let us review our current circumstances - and press on with this programme of actions and decisions.

Assuming that you have been following the **Actions** sections at the end of each of the foregoing chapters, you will have integrated yourself already into one of the anonymous fellowships and you will have provided yourself with a sponsor – either temporary or more permanent.

The programme does not absolutely require that you do Step Five with your sponsor. This is what it says:

Step Five:
We admitted to God, to ourselves, and to another human being the exact nature of our wrongs.

For a number of reasons it is customary, in the anonymous fellowships, to undertake your Step Five with your sponsor. In treatment centres, practices vary. Sometimes an experienced member of one of the anonymous fellowships is brought in from outside to hear a patient's Step Five. Sometimes, if the patient so wishes, a priest, minister or other religious functionary comes in for the purpose. In one of the treatment centres where I was once a patient, a former monk had been appointed 'Spiritual Counsellor' - and it was he who usually listened to each patient's Step Five. In the subterranean shrine which had been set aside for these purposes, he dozed gently throughout my own recitation. I did not find it particularly helpful.

On the other hand, when I later had to repeat Steps Four and Five in the outside world with my excellent sponsor, I found myself confronted with the opposite problem. My sponsor was *too* thorough for my liking. I wanted to storm through my list of resentments, scarcely pausing for breath. I thought that I understood fully the significance and implications of each one. I was impatient when he insisted on pausing and examining the circumstances, analysing my reactions and refuting some of my own conclusions. I had hoped to be shot of the damn thing in an hour or two at most. In fact, it took several visits and many hours of discussion before he was satisfied that I had a proper grip on Steps Four and Five. Uncharacteristically (he is usually a blithe, easygoing, happy-go-lucky sort of sponsor) he insisted on being painstaking and thorough. I am now very glad that he did – although at the time, as I have said, I found it irksome.

"I want what I want when I want it – which is now!" is the motto of the addict. This applies not just to the instant gratifications of active addiction. It is an attitude which often persists into recovery. In my own case, it meant that I wanted all of the benefits which recovery brings – but I was sometimes reluctant to put in the hard work which is the necessary precursor to these gains. Fortunately, by a mixture of humour, firmness and tact, my sponsor was able to keep my nose to the grindstone and my elbow to the wheel. It is a method which I try to use nowadays with my own patients and 'sponsees'.

There are a number of difficult 'issues' which may arise in connection with Step Five. The first of these is sex. Because some of the material in your Step Four schema will inevitably touch on this area, it is imperative that your relationship with the recipient of your **Step Five** should **not** be complicated by any sexual or romantic tensions. A practice much frowned on in the fellowships (but not, unhappily, unknown) is sometimes referred to as 'Thirteenth Stepping'. There is, of course, no thirteenth Step. The term denotes, rather, the formation of a romantic or sexual attachment between a relative newcomer and a more experienced member – who ought to know better. Avoid it.

All romantic and sexual relationships, in early recovery, are a dangerous distraction and lead to more relapses than almost any other cause. They can also be an addiction in themselves. I shall return to this question in Chapter 13 (Step Eight). For now, it is enough to note that it is unlikely that we shall be well enough to cope with *any* new romantic or sexual relationships until we have completed our Step Eight and have embarked upon Step Nine. Thankfully it is also true that, once we are well, our relationships will be better than anything we have previously known.

A second issue which may arise in connection with Step Five, is trust. It is to be hoped that, by now, you will have developed a relationship of solid trust with your sponsor – that you feel that there is not much, if anything, that you would not be prepared to discuss with him or her. If, for some reason (either to do with you, or to do with your sponsor), this is not the case, you could always consider doing your Step Five with a professional counsellor, with a priest or other clergyman – or even with a complete stranger, whom you will probably never see again in your life. There are, of course, both advantages and disadvantages to each of these recourses. The simple act of unburdening yourself to *someone* will probably afford you some relief. But it is clearly desirable that the recipient of your Step Five should have some idea of what you are trying to achieve – and it is even better if they themselves have undergone a similar process and have some knowledge of the purposes, in terms of the Programme, which this Step is designed to fulfil.

I now believe that there is a very profound psychological (or even spiritual) significance to the performance of Step Five. I do not wish to dwell upon this here, because the principal importance of this Step lies in the actions themselves and in their effects in the life of the individual. Step Five helps to free us from the things which have bound us. I think it entirely possible that this effect is not solely ascribable to the process which I mentioned in the preceding chapter. It does seem to be the case that, when we bring into the light those things which we have diligently cloaked in darkness, they lose their power over us. But there may well be another dimension to this mechanism. C.J. Jung's understanding of the operations of the unconscious included not only the unconscious mind of the individual, but also what he called 'the collective unconscious'. Classical Freudian doctrine assumes that unconscious processes may sometimes perform a healing function. The tensions and contradictions of our waking life are somehow balanced, reconciled and healed through dreams and other operations of the unconscious mind. Is it possible that Jung's 'collective unconscious' may perform a similar function? Is it further possible that the conflicts and tensions of our waking life cannot enter the realm of the collective unconscious *until we communicate them to at least one other human being*? These are beguiling questions to which, as yet, there are no definitive answers. Psychology, as a science, is still in its infancy. The little we do know about the human psyche is insignificant by comparison with all that remains unknown.

Be that as it may, what is empirically certain is that, for whatever reason, Step Five *works*. I have found, simply as a matter of observation, that, for most people, Step Five has a profound and liberating effect.

I have also found, however, that, as with many other spiritual events, the effect is not always instantaneous. It often takes about three days to 'gel'. Do not therefore expect, necessarily, to feel an overwhelming and immediate sense of release as soon as you have completed your Step Five. Some people do. But do not be surprised if, during a short period after completion of your Step Five, you are assailed by doubts and regrets at having undertaken such a comprehensive measure of self-disclosure. This is not unusual – and soon passes. If you have chosen well the recipient of your Step Five, your confidences will never be imparted to any third person. Within the fellowships, it is well understood that the confidentiality of Step Five is as sacrosanct as the Seal of Confession in the Catholic Church. Look after yourself well during this brief interim. Be kind to yourself – but don't 'use'! It would be a pretty lousy 'reward' for all your hard work.

In one of the treatment centres with which I am familiar there was a charming and useful custom. On completion of Step Five, each patient had a 'burning ceremony'.

In a secluded area of the garden stood a brazier. As darkness fell, the new 'graduate' went with his or her peers to this special place. And there, with the singing of songs, the emblems of a former life were burned. Blazing fragments of paperwork, usually including Step Four, rose glowing into the darkening sky. At my own ceremony, I had to burn the tattered fur coat, to which you were introduced in Chapter 2.! Unfortunately, I believe that the bureaucrats, with their endless Health and Safety Regulations, have now put a stop to this admirable symbolic rite in treatment centres. But there is nothing to prevent you from arranging your own, private 'burning ceremony'.

You may find it useful, however, to hang on to your Step Four paperwork for the time being. It can be a helpful reference source in the work which remains to be done.

ACTIONS   10.

*Just as, in Step Four, we took **our own** moral inventory (not anyone else's), so here, in **Step Five** we admit the wrongs **which we have done** to others and to ourselves. We do **not** rehearse the wrongs which we believe others have done to us.*

10. a.   Choose someone to hear your Step Five – normally your Sponsor.

10. b.   Arrange a mutually convenient time (or times – it may require more than one visit).

10. c.   Keep the appointments. Take your Step Four schema and written notes with you.

10. d.   Discuss thoroughly everything in your Step Four work (and anything else which arises or which still troubles you).

Congratulations! You have completed Step Five.

NB
*If, after completing your Step Five, you remember other matters which you feel you should have mentioned, do not worry. All such material can be 'mopped up' in **Step Ten**.*

11. PREPARING FOR CHANGE – STEP SIX

Steps Six and Seven are sometimes referred to as the 'forgotten Steps'. They are passed over quite quickly in the AA 'Big Book' and, on the whole, are not so much talked about, within the Fellowships, as some of the more 'spectacular' Steps. I now believe that they are absolutely crucial and deserve far more attention than they usually receive.

There is absolutely no point in persisting with recovery, unless it enables us to become whole, happy, healed individuals. I personally would not bother with recovery if it was simply a grim daily struggle of self-denial and abstinence. If I am going to be just as miserable in recovery as I was when I was 'using', I might as well continue using. I already know how to make myself and other people miserable. If recovery is simply going to be more of the same, I might as well be miserable with my drugs and drink.

One cold winter, many years ago, I found myself living in a Church Army hostel in a certain city. My habits and haunts were now very different from the gilded lifestyle I had enjoyed around Knightsbridge and Chelsea in my youth. The large dormitory on the first floor of the ramshackle hostel was packed with creaking iron bedsteads which looked as though they had been acquired second-hand from Florence Nightingale's casualty ward in the Crimea. At night, before going to sleep, it was necessary to attach our few possessions to our persons with bits of wire and scraps of string. Without this precaution, by the morning, they would certainly have been 'lifted' by unknown hands. We all slept with our boots on. I once put a cheap alarm-clock well under the thin horse-hair mattress. By the morning it was gone. All of us lived by petty-pilfering and Social Security payments – and, popular mythology notwithstanding, there is no honour among thieves. Addiction ultimately makes thieves of all who are in its grip.

During the day we were all turned out to wander the streets and in the evenings we were readmitted to be given a basic meal. At night the cacophony of snoring and farts made sleep difficult. The stench was dreadful. But it was at least warm in the hostel – and I considered it luxurious by comparison with the open-ended concrete pipe on a vacant lot which had been my previous dwelling.

By this point in my long decline I had neither the money nor the personal resourcefulness to acquire illegal drugs very often. For the most part, alcohol had become my drug of choice. I had discovered that it was far more efficacious when supplemented with benzodiazepines (diazepam, lorazepam etc.) and chlormethiazole (Heminevrin). Prescriptions for these were easily extracted from kindly local practitioners and the drugs were munificently distributed, free of charge, from local pharmacies to anyone who was receiving Social Security benefits. I thought the National Health Service was wonderful.

To help to fill the grey, empty daylight hours, I sometimes shuffled along to the local drug and alcohol dependency service. They had a 'drop-in' centre where, out of the cold wind, piping hot tea was always on tap. There were even some smart-looking counsellors. I began to see one on a regular basis. He was a brisk young man with a first-class honours degree in psychology from a redbrick university. He said that I was going to be weaned away from my illegal drugs – but that I could still have prescribed drugs. He was even going to teach me 'controlled drinking'. This all seemed to me to be a marvellous idea. Just what I had been looking for. He used sonorous and inspiring phrases like 'motivational interviewing', 'cognitive behavioural therapy', 'harm-minimisation' and 'rehabilitative medication maintenance'. He promised to show me how to lead a hassle-free and productive life, *without* having to give up my drink and drugs. It was perfect. I embarked with enthusiasm upon the measures which he proposed.

I learned all about my 'trigger' situations and how to cope with them. I learned how many 'units' of alcohol I could safely allow myself each day. I learned of all the dangers attendant upon uncontrolled use of drink and drugs. I learned about 'crisis-management'. I learned that it was possible for me to hold down a simple job while still on medication. I learned how to restore my relations with others to a better footing. I learned how to cope with cravings. I learned how to recognise my own faulty thinking and beliefs. I learned how to *behave* differently. Outwardly, my life began to improve.

There was only one problem. I was still utterly miserable. It was a complete bloody nightmare. The 'units' of alcohol and the prescribed medications were never enough. I was just as preoccupied with drink and drug related concerns as I had ever been. Whereas, previously, my every waking moment had been dominated by the necessities of getting and using my drugs and alcohol, now my life was totally dominated by 'controlling' these factors. I had not been freed of obsession. I had simply replaced one set of obsessions with a different, but equally demoralising, set of obsessions. I had learned how to function better – but my life was more restricted, more joyless, more monochrome, more grinding than ever. This was not freedom and recovery. This was drudgery. I longed for sunlight and laughter. But all I had was earnestness, frustration and angst.

I now know the reason for this. My behaviours had changed considerably – but *I* had not changed in any fundamental way. For me, outward behavioural change had not been accompanied by inner, personal change – and it had certainly not solved the inward spiritual problem. It had alleviated some of the symptoms and consequences of my addictive disorders – but it had in no way treated my underlying addictive disease.

Needless to say, as soon as I had saved up a bit of money, I said to myself "Fuck that!" and went on an enormous 'bender' of drinking and drugging. Even the outward gains soon vanished. I soon lost my job, split up with my girlfriend, broke my collar-bone and wound up in a mental hospital. Despite all my newly-acquired knowledge, I was as spiritually bankrupt as ever.

To become happy and spiritually well, we need to do more than changing some of our behaviours. Step Six points us towards some of the changes which will be needed. This is what it says:

Step Six

We were entirely ready to have God remove all these defects of character.

Let's try to see what this means, in practice.

Before God, or anyone else, can remove our defects of character we need to know what they are. Steps Four and Five should already have given us a pretty clear idea of some of the factors which have been impeding our progress. The pioneers of recovery draw particular attention to a relatively small number of characteristics which, in the past, may have prevented us from conducting our lives in a rewarding and satisfying way. Fear, selfishness, resentment, envy, self-will, dishonesty, *hubris* (unwarranted pride), self-pity, insecurity and an unwillingness to take responsibility for our own lives are among the most common. These defects, of course, are not the exclusive preserve of those who have addictive disease. But, for us, they are particularly corrosive and they are intensified and accentuated by active addiction. They are also the characteristics which most commonly bring us into conflict and collision with others. Moreover, the more deeply embedded they become in our personalities, the more difficult it is for us to get well – and the more readily we can lead ourselves back into active addiction.

Although I prefer to keep this book free of 'case histories', as far as possible, a brief illustration of this point may be useful here. It is not a particularly unusual or startling case – but it is nevertheless very instructive. A young man, let us call him Peter, had turned up at a treatment centre where I was on the staff. He was about twenty-five years old and had been brought in by his parents, who were in despair. Peter, who was still living at his parents' modest home, had become completely addicted to heroin. For two or three nightmarish years his parents had been sucked into this world. When he ran out of drugs, Peter became angry, abusive and violent. Sometimes he stole from his parents or from their house. At other times he went out and committed other crimes to fund his addiction. He kept getting arrested and had already spent six months in prison. As soon as he was released, he went straight round to his dealer and was soon using more heroin than he had been before his incarceration. At one point, his mother became so desperate to protect her son and the family's good name that she herself used to go out to 'score' for him. She visited the dealers and bought his drugs for him with her own slender housekeeping money.

With infinite patience, and by keeping him at home, Peter had been gradually weaned off his heroin. His parents had brought him to the treatment centre *not* for treatment of his heroin addiction, but for benzodiazepine addiction. He had apparently become addicted to benzodiazepines, prescribed by his doctor. Peter and his parents were loud in their condemnation of this doctor. He should never have prescribed these drugs, they said. It was *his* fault that Peter had got addicted again. The doctor was to blame. He should be struck-off, they said. He should be sued.

Let us stand back for a moment and look at what was really going on here. As usual, at the centre of the *maelstrom* is an addict – in this case, Peter. By a combination of emotional blackmail and manipulation (we are usually very good at this) Peter has managed to get his parents running around for him, feeding his habit, enabling him in every possible way. To achieve this end he is pretending that he has stopped using heroin. Actually, as blood-tests soon confirm, he is still using heroin *as well as* benzodiazepines. When I question him about how he got started on the benzodiazepines, this is what he says:

"It was that bloody doctor. He gave them to me."

"Yes. But *why* did he give them to you?"

"I dunno. He's stupid."

"Why did you go and see the doctor?"

"I had a sore throat. My throat was very sore. I could hardly speak."

"So he prescribed benzos for your sore throat?"

"Yeah. Well, no. He gave me some antibiotics."

"So what were the benzos for?"

"I told him I was nervy and couldn't sleep."

"What else did you tell him?"

"I said I just needed something to tide me over."

It is becoming clear that Peter has manipulated the doctor to get his prescriptions and it later emerges that he has a history of doing this. And yet his resentment against the doctor is not wholly feigned. His disease presents the circumstances to him in this light. At this point, he really does see himself as a victim - and he has got his parents playing the same game. This warped and distorted thinking is very characteristic of addiction. It is built into our denial-systems. It can become very deeply ingrained.

Later on in his treatment, Peter was able to see how dishonest he had been with himself and how he had manipulated his parents, the doctors and everyone else around him. He acknowledged that his selfishness and fear of being without drugs had resulted in his mother going out to buy drugs for him. He began to take responsibility for his own actions and decisions. His resentment against the doctor dissolved and he began to shed the underlying attitude of self-pity and victimhood.

Equally important was the realisation by Peter's parents that, by protecting him from the natural consequences of his addiction and by continually blaming others, they had enabled Peter to avoid responsibility for his own recovery. With the best of intentions, they had 'enabled' him to stay sick. As long as others are running around, bailing us out, clearing up our messes, paying our debts and making excuses for us, we have no incentive to get well. It was not until my own parents finally stopped doing this and put me on a train with a one-way ticket for London (telling me that, henceforth, I was on my own) that I began, gradually and in sheer desperation, to do what was necessary to get well. I did not thank them for it at the time! But, now, I am extremely grateful.

This is all part of the essential work of Step Six. Our defects of character cannot be removed until we begin to recognise them for what they are. But Step Six takes us further. To be rid of these warped, distorted and selfish attitudes we must be ready to let them go. This is not quite as easy as it sounds. Logically, one might think that, as soon as we discover that particular attitudes are not helpful to us, we would be only too glad to be shot of them. However, all people are creatures of habit – and addicts more so than most. We do not like to let go of habits of mind which are familiar to us – even when we know that they are impeding our progress. If we have constructed a world in which we see ourselves as victims of bad luck, of circumstances, of the malevolence or stupidity of others – and then the foundations of this world are shaken – we fear that we may fall into the abyss.

Many other psychological approaches to the problem of addiction can teach us how to be relatively abstinent for a while – Cognitive Behaviour Therapy (CBT), Rational Emotive Behavioural Therapy (REBT), Reality Therapy and Choice Theory, Motivational Interviewing, Transactional Analysis (TA), Psychosynthesis, Person-Centred Therapy, Neuro-Linguistic Programming (NLP) - the list of theories is endless and ever-multiplying. Some of these approaches may even teach us how to change our thinking about our problems. But I have not yet come across convincing evidence that any of these methodologies, of themselves, can produce the fundamental changes of attitude (and in the personality) which are required for a contented and sustained recovery. Such methodologies may take away our substances and processes of choice on a temporary, or even quite lasting, basis – but they do not replace them with anything meaningful. They help us to dismantle our old *weltanschauüng* (world-view) but they leave us teetering on the edge of the abyss. However, because this simple 12 Step programme is not merely psychological, but spiritual, in emphasis, it is capable of filling this void. Diligently pursued, it will replace our old, unworkable ideas with new and satisfying values – new and workable principles by which to live. Long after all these acronyms have gone the way of the therapeutic fads which preceded them, the Twelve Step Programme will still be producing miracles of recovery.

For each and every one of the defects which we may have noticed in our previous lives (fear, selfishness, resentment, envy, self-will, dishonesty, *hubris*, insecurity, self-pity, unwillingness to take responsibility for ourselves etc.) there is a countervailing positive quality which we are now free to develop. In Chapter 12, which deals with Step Seven, we shall say more about *how* we can cultivate these countervailing qualities and attitudes.

There is a pernicious and ubiquitous old myth that you cannot teach an old dog new tricks. It may well be true that, as we grow older, it becomes more difficult for us to acquire new technical skills. Someone who has shown no mathematical aptitude before the age of twenty-five is unlikely to become an Einstein. But these restrictions do not seem to apply in the spiritual and ethical realms. Our values can and do change throughout our lives. It only remains for us to ensure that they change *for the better*.

The most remarkable – and apparently miraculous – transformations can occur in people of every age. Everybody who is in recovery *knows* this to be true. It is a fact of our daily experience. If you speak to people whose lives have been transformed in this way, many of them will tell you that Steps Six and Seven are among the most significant influences which contribute to this change.

ACTIONS   11.

We do not need to worry, yet, about whether God, or anyone else, is going to be able to 'remove our defects of character'. All we need to do, for now, is to become aware of what these defects are – and to become 'ready' to let them go. If I am determined to cling on to my defects, nothing and nobody can remove them.

However, a number of points need to be made in relation to defects of character. The first of these may seem obvious, but is still worth stressing:

We make our own diagnosis.

*Our discussions with our sponsor may have been helpful in highlighting certain characteristics which seem to have been causing us problems. But nobody, either within the fellowships or without, is in a position to enumerate our faults. Our spouses, parents or employers may have strong views on these questions – and there are times when we need to be open-minded enough to consider such points of view. But, unless we can see for ourselves that adjustments are required, our willingness to relinquish our negative attitudes will be half-hearted, at best. Above all, we should not assume that messages and descriptions received from childhood onwards are necessarily accurate. "You're bad tempered", "You're stupid", "You're wicked", "You're lazy", "You'll never amount to anything" are the kind of phrases which may have been instilled into us from a very early age. We need to break free of all this and to make **our own** honest appraisal.*

*The second point which needs to be made in connection with defects of character is that they do not and cannot exist in a vacuum. They are expressed through specific actions and patterns of behaviour in the real world. They are usually exemplified in our relations and interactions **with other people**.*

Thirdly, and finally, we should remind ourselves again of the dangers of perfectionism. We need to avoid excessive zeal in seeking out our imperfections. We need to be clearsighted and honest – but nothing is to be gained from 'beating ourselves up'. The purpose of identifying our shortcomings is not to engage in an orgy of self-castigation. The ultimate purpose is that we should be set free.

In Steps Four and Five, we have looked extensively at our former lives and we have identified a number of behaviours, attitudes and characteristics which have been unhelpful to us in the past. Let us now turn to the present. In the here and now, let us ask ourselves this question:

11. a.

*To what extent are my actions **still** governed by selfishness, self-pity, resentment, envy, fear, insecurity, self-will, and the desire to blame other people? Do any of these characteristics **still** poison my relationships, when I think of all the people who feature in my life today?*

*Conflicts with other people are not always or necessarily an indication that our own character defects are at work – but they are a good place to start to look, especially when such conflicts are prolonged. We addicts and alcoholics are not the only people in the world who are spiritually sick, alas. But, individually, we **are** the only people whose sickness we can personally address. Let's look at any situations where we currently find ourselves in conflict with others and let's look at **our own part** in producing or prolonging those conflicts. Let's get it all down on paper. Here are some hypothetical examples. You might like to make a grid and put in your own examples.*

With **whom** am I in conflict – and **why**?	What defects in my own character are contributing to this situation?
Becky – my line manager. She's an ignorant, idle trollop. She knows less about her job than I do. She refused to implement the changes I suggested. I think she told the boss that I'm troublesome.	**Self-will** - I want to get my own way over this issue. **Self-pity** - I feel undervalued. **Hubris** – I think I know better than her. **Insecurity** (fear) – I might lose my job. **Resentment**
My bank manager. He's unreasonable. He refused to increase my overdraft limit. He's stupid. He can't see the advantages of the scheme I'm proposing.	**Insecurity** – he might demand the money I owe him. Fear. **Hubris** – I think my financial judgment is better than his. **Self-will** – I'm angry because my personal comfort and convenience are threatened.
My sister, Laura. She's a selfish cow. She never does anything for anybody. She keeps dumping her children on me and she never helps our parents. She never does anything for me. She doesn't know how lucky she is. *Etc.*	**Self-pity** – I feel like a victim in this situation. I always end up having to do everything. **Envy** – I secretly wish I could be as strong-minded as her. I wouldn't mind having her lifestyle. *Etc.*

*Notice that, in drawing-up our schema, we are **not** making any judgment about who is right or wrong in each situation. It may well be that my financial judgment really **is** better than my bank manager's – although it is unlikely. We are simply examining the negative feelings which arise from the situation and which may be causing or prolonging the conflict. We are trying to identify personality traits in ourselves which disturb our own tranquillity and prevent us from enjoying our lives.*

In the next chapter we shall be examining some of the ways in which we can be released from these impediments.

The list of defects which I have given above is by no means exhaustive. You will doubtless be able to pinpoint your own most besetting faults. Some people like to use the traditional 'seven deadly sins' as a starting point.

Anger, you will have noticed, is absent above. This is because anger is usually a reaction to fear. It is a secondary, not a primary emotion. We get angry when we, or our plans, are threatened in some way. Sometimes, our fear and anger have their roots, not in the present, but in the past. If, therefore, we can resolve the fear problem, the anger will diminish of its own accord.

11. b.

In the place where you live, go through all your things - and chuck out all the stuff you never use.

If it's just junk, sling it out. If it's saleable, sell it – or give it to a charity shop. This gives us excellent practice in 'letting go' of things.

By now, you will be very familiar with the prayer which concludes most meetings in the anonymous fellowships. 'God grant me the serenity to accept the things I cannot change, courage to change the things I can - and the wisdom to know the difference'.

*My first sponsor used to say that most of the things we **cannot** change are to do with other people. If we keep trying to change other people we* *are doomed to frustration and despondency. Most of the things we **can** change, he said, are to do with ourselves.*

As a counsellor, I have particular reason to know that this is true. I cannot change anybody. The most that I can do is to suggest to patients ways in which they can change themselves. And I can continue making my own changes. We strive for progress – not perfection.

12.   WORKING WITH CHANGE – STEP SEVEN

"Be careful what you pray for. You might get it." So runs a useful admonition sometimes heard in the Fellowships.

Prayer, when we pray aright, works. I don't know why it works, but it does. I have seen it work for others and I have known it to work for me. There are a number of possible explanations for this. Some say that it is a purely psychological matter: that prayer helps to focus our mental energies towards particular ends which are therefore more likely to be encompassed. Others say that it works by direct divine intervention in response to our prayers. Nowadays, I incline towards *both* views. We shall return later to the question of what is meant by 'praying aright'.

For most people who are in recovery there comes a point at which it is no longer possible to dodge the issue of a 'Higher Power'. In early recovery, it is quite sufficient that we should recognise that the power of a group or team of people is greater than the power of a lone individual – both in dealing with this disease and in many other fields of endeavour. Most of us do not have much difficulty in acknowledging that the power inherent in this programme of recovery has worked for countless people who had not been able to help themselves. Such individuals and teams are to be found in the Anonymous Fellowships throughout the world. But it is also clear that the originators of this Programme had something rather more than this in mind when they spoke of a 'Higher Power'. If we look at Steps 3, 5, 6 and 11 we shall find that the very contentious word 'God' is used quite explicitly.

For most people who enter recovery as agnostics or even (as I once was) as militant atheists, there is a gradual recognition of a power greater than themselves. Confronted by the evidence of our own helplessness and of our apparently miraculous recoveries, we are forced to admit that we have been given something which we were never able to achieve on our own. Some people eventually choose to call the source of this healing 'God'. For others, what the AA 'Big Book' calls 'God-consciousness' remains very much more tentative. For some, its onset appears to be very gradual indeed. For yet others, it may be sudden, intense and overwhelming.

I make no evaluation here of the validity or of the reality of such experiences. Indeed, to attempt to do so would be presumptuous. However, irrespective of the means by which people arrive at a more theistic interpretation of their lives and of the world, we here note only that many **do** conclude that there is a 'God' *of some sort.* Some go further. They come to believe in an omnipotent deity who, through the mighty laws of nature perceived and described by science, creates and sustains the entire universe.

To those who *are* able to arrive at such a view it seems reasonable to suppose that, since persons are a part of the created order, one aspect of that deity must also be personal. Nor does it seem too preposterous to such believers to accept that a being who creates and sustains a universe is also able to intervene in that universe at any level. They believe, in short, in the possibility of miracles. For many others, of course, there is neither empirical nor experiential evidence sufficient to justify such a leap of faith.

What is certain, nevertheless, is that, if we wish to succeed in recovering from addiction, we must change very profoundly. I often reiterate to patients who arrive in the treatment centre where I work that, if we leave treatment fundamentally the same people as we were when we first came into treatment, there is a strong probability that, sooner or later, we shall find ourselves doing the same kind of things. We shall find ourselves back in Gomorrah. Recovery, I repeat, is therefore primarily about change. Whether we regard the changes necessary for recovery as the products of external interventions or of our own internal processes (or of both), it is obviously helpful if we ourselves co-operate in such alterations. It is very difficult for anyone or anything to change me very fundamentally, if I do not wish to be changed. As we noted in our consideration of Step Six, nothing and nobody can remove my defects of character if I am grimly determined to hang on to them. Somehow, I must develop the *willingness* to let them go and be free of them.

Step Seven runs as follows:

We humbly asked God to remove our shortcomings.

We have dealt, I think, sufficiently with the question of what is meant by 'God' in this context. Everyone arrives at their own understanding of this term. There are, however, three cognate questions which present themselves as a consequence of what has been said above. The first relates to the 'turning of the will'. The second has to do with the nature of humility. The third concerns what we mean by 'praying aright'.

It seems to me that what we loosely term the human 'will' may be subdivided into at least two kinds. We should distinguish between what may be termed the 'conscious' will, on the one hand, and the will of the unconscious mind, on the other. Indeed, it may well be that the problem of the ineffectuality of 'will-power' in counteracting addictive disease arises precisely from our failure to distinguish between these different sorts of 'will'. The conscious will may be designated as that set of intentions and decisions which is generated by cognitive processes. It relates to what classical Freudian metaphor would describe as the operations of the Ego. In the metaphor of Transactional Analysis, it would signify the processes initiated by the Adult. But it would seem that there is another 'will' – a deeper and more primeval will.

Madonna once made an atrocious film. It was so bad that, now, I do not even remember the name of it. In this film, she finds herself (in the traditional and improbable cliché) marooned on a desert island with an extremely unconvincing and disagreeable 'stud'. A corny and predictable 'relationship' ensues. But there is *one* good and memorable line in the movie. At a certain point, Madonna, in speaking of her former life as a venal, materialistic bitch, says "…but the things I wanted were not good for me". This states succinctly one of the essential dichotomies of addiction. The things we want are not good for us. In our conscious minds, we know this. But still we want them. We really *want* them – at a powerful visceral level, beyond the reach of conscious thought or choice. In Freudian terms, it is our Id that wants these things. In the language of TA, it is our Child that demands them. Our need for our substances and processes of choice may be compared to the need of an infant to be suckled. Indeed, addiction may involve a distorted development of this very need.

Viewed in these terms, the conflict between our desire to be free of our addiction and the imperative demand for instant gratification becomes more comprehensible. On a conscious, cognitive level we desire recovery and all of its long-term benefits. But our infantile nature (our Child or Id) knows nothing of the long-term – and cares even less. It knows only that pleasurable feelings result from certain actions. One of our tasks, therefore, as we progress in our recovery, may be seen as the 'turning of the will'. Somehow, we must bring our unconscious, instinctual will into conformity with our conscious desires and intentions. It is one of the paradoxes of addiction that we may have the conscious *will* to be rid of our 'defects of character' – but yet lack the *willingness* to relinquish them.

This is perhaps why therapies which depend solely on conscious, cognitive processes have only limited and temporary success in the treatment of addiction.

My first sponsor once taught me that, before we pray for the *ability* to do something, it is sometimes necessary to pray for the *willingness*. Let me illustrate this point with the actual case. I was having trouble with cigarettes. Cigarette-smoking was chronologically the first of my active addictions. I smoked cigarettes addictively long before I picked up my other substances and processes of addiction. This addiction also persisted longer than most of the other manifestations of my addictive disease. It was, in many senses, more deeply embedded than any of the other addictive behaviours - because it was associated with virtually every action and event of my daily life. If the telephone rang, I had to have a cigarette. With a cup of tea, I had to have a cigarette. After a meal; cigarette. Writing a letter; cigarette. Trying to seduce someone; cigarette (perhaps this is why I was not very successful!). It was more difficult to dislodge than my other addictions – and it 'saw me through' all of them. I smoked throughout the earlier part of my recovery from other drugs and alcohol. Only when I reached Step Six did I begin, at my sponsor's suggestion, to regard this (and one or two other addictive/compulsive behaviours) as amongst my 'defects of character'.

By this time I had overcome my objections to prayer – so I prayed long and earnestly to be rid of these enslavements. But nothing happened. And nothing continued to happen. I sometimes managed to reduce the number of cigarettes I smoked each day. But never for long. Occasionally, I stopped smoking altogether – for a day or two, at most. This continued until I remembered my sponsor's advice.

Then I realised that, although I had the conscious *will* to stop smoking, I did not have the *willingness* to do it. So I began to pray for willingness. Gradually, it worked. Gradually, my instinctual, unconscious will came into conformity with my conscious, cognitive will (and both, it is to be hoped, came into conformity with the 'divine' will). I reduced the number of cigarettes I was smoking until it was only three or four a day (at one time, I had smoked 60 Capstan Full Strength per day!). At this low level, I realised that the amount of actual nicotine which I was ingesting daily was negligible. It was no longer a physiological dependency. It was simply a compulsive process. So I stopped it. Such is the power of prayer. So far (one day at a time) I have not picked them up again.

I have sometimes been asked whether the use, in some treatment centres, of the twelve-step recovery programme in the treatment of various sexual addictions and compulsions indicates that it might profitably be used in the treatment of today's most prevalent legal, moral and psychiatric preoccupation – paedophilia.

The honest answer is: I do not know. For, although I have had patients who have admitted to an erotic interest in photographs of naked children (which, incidentally, seems to be more common than one might suppose), this addiction to child-pornography has usually been of a secondary nature - a 'cross-addiction' from the primary addictive manifestation (alcoholism, cocaine-use, heroin addiction, etc.). In the histories of many patients there are often reported incidents (usually during adolescence) of sexual contacts with individuals both very much older and very much younger than themselves. This, indeed, is so common that it may be possible to regard it simply as part of the sexual experimentation often associated with adolescence. When, however, these behaviours persist into adulthood, they may justly be regarded as pathological. I personally have not yet had occasion to treat active paedophilia as a primary addiction.

Theoretically, however, the application of these principles ought to be of benefit in such cases. Paedophilia exhibits all of the characteristics which are commonly held to define addictions (preoccupation, protection of supply, secretive use, mood-altering effects, denial etc., etc.) It exhibits them all to an extreme and damaging degree. There is no doubt in my mind that paedophilia is, among other things, an addictive process. The fundamental processes of the twelve-step programme of recovery (abstinence accompanied by spiritual change) *ought*, therefore, to have a salutary effect. But that is the most that can be said.

As with any other addictive disorder, continuing abstinence is conditional on the daily maintenance of spiritual health. This programme has never claimed to 'cure' any of the addictive disorders. In order to keep his or her insanity at bay, the addict must take responsibility for continuing to practise these principles (including Steps 6 & 7) on a daily basis. Just as with any other addiction, therefore, in the case of paedophilia, relapse, with all of its dreadful consequences to so many lives, is unfortunately always possible.

In a more general way, it may be apposite at this point (and in connection with Step Seven) to reiterate what has already been said in respect of some of the previous Steps. *This programme is cumulative, not merely sequential.* We cannot 'do' a Step – and then simply forget about it. As we shall see, when we come to discuss Step Twelve, we are enjoined to 'practise these principles in all our affairs'. Nevertheless, there is often a first and 'formal' occasion upon which we commit ourselves to a particular Step. And this is what we are about to do with Step Seven.

ACTIONS   *12.*

12. a.

Having extracted, in Step Six, a serviceable list of our main defects from our current conflicts with others, let us now supplement it with it any additional flaws of which we may be aware. Armed with this list, let us go to our sponsor and discuss each item with him or her. As with Step Three, I know of no better way to commit ourselves to Step Seven than that recommended in the most seminal work of recovery.

12. b.

In your AA 'Big Book' find the Step Seven Prayer. Write it out in your own words until you and your sponsor are satisfied. You should, by now, be beginning to develop a clearer idea of what the words 'Higher Power' or 'God' might mean to you personally.

12. c.

*Either on your knees, or in any other posture which accords with your own belief system, say the prayer together with your sponsor. Remember, however, what this Step actually says: 'We **humbly** asked God to remove our shortcomings'. Humility should never be confused with humiliation. Humility is simply the recognition of our proper location in the greater order. It is acquired through the insight into our limitations and potentialities which is vouchsafed by practising conscientiously **all** of the preceding Steps.*

*"God" says the old axiom "helps those who help themselves". **Not** doing something is very much harder than doing something else instead. If, then, we have been able to identify our own most besetting faults, we should consciously set about practising the opposite 'virtues'. Patience for impatience. Selflessness for selfishness. Industry for sloth, etc.*

Letting go of our defects and acquiring new and useful characteristics are processes which we shall almost certainly need to practice on a daily basis for the rest of our lives. God may well remove some of my defects occasionally. But God only seems to do so for the duration of, at most, one day! The following morning they are usually back again in full force. That is why I have to renew my Step Seven on a daily basis.

13.   OTHER PEOPLE'S PAIN – STEP EIGHT

I married my first wife when we were both in our very early twenties – and I proceeded to turn her life into a living nightmare. My addictive disease was already far advanced. I did not know how sick I was - and I did not wish to know.

She, poor girl, had no experience of addiction and could not know what she had let herself in for. I played a grim game of emotional 'brinkmanship' with her. My own conduct took me to the brink and beyond. I pushed *her* to the brink and beyond. I had an immature and egotistical belief that, no matter how appallingly I behaved towards her, she should give me 'unconditional' love. And, bless her, for years *she did*.

Eventually, while I was in a clinic being detoxified, she went off to Germany with a Dutchman.

Despite my own previous infidelities, I collapsed into a snivelling heap of wounded feelings and nauseating self-pity, tearfully recounting the tale of her treachery to anyone who would listen. In reality, I had played for rejection – but was staggered and appalled when I got it.

Today, I am not surprised that she left me. In fact, I am astonished that she put up with me for as long as she did. I stole from her much of her youth. The devotion which may be displayed by the partners of people with addictive disease is often no less than heroic. But, with the best of intentions, they often enable us to remain sick.

This is what **Step Eight** says:
We made a list of all persons we had harmed, and became willing to make amends to them all.

My first wife's name is now on my list of the people to whom I am *willing* to make amends – but it took a very long time to get there. For years, I genuinely believed that it was *I* who was the injured party! Moreover, the fact that she is now on my list does not necessarily mean that I shall ever attempt to make any *direct* amend to her. Quite apart from the fact that any effort to make an amend is bound to be totally inadequate to the case, it may never be appropriate to attempt a *direct* amend. As we shall see when we come to consider **Step Nine**, it may well be that the best amend I can make to her is to stay out of her present life altogether. It is enough, for now, that I am *willing* to make a fitting amend (however inadequate it may be) – if a suitable occasion should ever arise.

There are, then, three very compelling reasons why we should not attempt to get to grips with Steps 8 and 9 until we have a thorough grounding in **all** the preceding Steps. Firstly, it is unlikely that we shall be able to recognise properly the harm that we have done to other people until our perspectives have been changed sufficiently by the preceding Steps. Secondly, our motives for wishing to make direct amends may not be quite as pure as the driven snow, if we have not been thorough in practising the first seven Steps. (This is especially the case when we come to consider past partners and lovers!) And, thirdly, our own judgment in each case is, in any case, likely to be somewhat defective. All of these conditions may still obtain – even when we *have* been practising the first seven Steps to the best of our ability. It is for this reason that it is vital that we continue to consult our Sponsor.

One of my sponsees, a heroin addict in recovery, suggested that it might be his duty to make amends to *all* of his former partners for the poor quality of their sex-life when he was in active addiction – by having sublime sex with them in recovery. Although, fortunately, he was joking, this is precisely the kind of sly, specious reasoning which we may sometimes employ to disguise selfish motives. We are usually quite good at cloaking our reprehensible intentions with fair and noble motives. And we do this as much to justify our actions *to ourselves* as to hoodwink others.

This brings us, fairly naturally, to the whole question of 'relationships' in recovery. There are some people who say that we must not engage in any *new* relationships, of a sexual or romantic nature, for at least a year after we get clean and sober. Others say not for two years. Yet others say eighteen months. Or six months. Or three years. From this great diversity of opinion, we may infer that part of the original premise is faulty. It is not so much an arbitrary measure of *time* which determines whether or not we are ready for a relationship – it is the *progress* we are making in our recovery. My own Sponsor suggested that it is not until we have done an Eighth Step (and have embarked upon our Ninth) that we are ready to contemplate the possibility of a new 'relationship'. At first I chose to ignore his advice – and later lived to regret it. With the benefit of hindsight, I can see why his original suggestion makes sense.

When we first embark upon recovery, our lives and relationships (of *all* kinds) are usually in a mess. We cannot even relate properly to *ourselves* at this point. What hope have we of forming a meaningful relationship with another human being? Many of us mistake neediness, desperation and dependency for 'love'. We are, by the very nature of our condition, extremely dependent people. And we have usually depended not only upon chemicals, substances and liquids to 'fix' us, physically and emotionally, but also upon *people*. We would do well to stop depending on people, places, substances and all *external* things to make us feel good about ourselves - and to start building up our own *inner* resilience. External 'props' fail us and disappear. Interior resources don't. Thus, there is a paradoxical sense in which we are not really ready for a 'relationship' – until we no longer desperately need one. I shall return to these points in the chapter which follows.

There are three important relationships which we need to get right before we can begin to relate properly to another human being on a healthy basis of intimacy.

Firstly, we need to begin to relate in a positive way to *ourselves*. If we don't much like ourselves, we will go into any relationship with the expectation that, sooner or later, the other person won't like us much either.

Secondly we need to build a constructive relationship with our Higher Power – whatever that may be. I remember a Pentecostalist preacher trying to help me when I was in active addiction who said, in his own idiom, "Get right with God!". I think I know, now, what he was driving at.

Thirdly, we need to relate appropriately to the generality of our fellow-addicts in recovery – and to our sponsor, in particular.

These new, productive relationships take time to grow – and they develop in tandem with our progress in the Steps. Before we can have successful and mutually rewarding relationships with other people – before, in fact, we can lead a satisfying life – most of us have a great deal of work to do on ourselves. How can we give this work the energy and priority it requires, if the greater part of our attention is focussed on somebody else? Indeed, this attempt to divert our attention may well be one of the ruses employed by our addictive disease to *prevent* us from getting well. It is a distraction which promises 'instant gratification'. It is yet another 'feelings fix' from an external source.

Similarly, before we enter into any new, committed 1/1 relationship, most of us have a great deal of work to do in resolving our *existing* relationships. Spouses, children, parents, employers, lovers, friends and relatives may all have been hurt by our chaotic behaviour in active addiction. It is one of the principal purposes of Steps Eight and Nine to set these matters right, as far as possible. Until we have done so, we cannot know what types of further relationships we shall be having – or with whom. We may be tempted to rush into a relationship with a new lover, thinking that we have completely burned our boats with our former partner – only to find that, once the poison of active addiction is removed, the marriage or partnership is healed.

It is also, however, not uncommon to find that a marriage or partnership whose dynamics have been dictated by addictive disease (in one or both partners) is no longer workable, once recovery enters the picture. This is especially the case where compulsive helping or compulsive controlling have played a part in the relationship. Most partners of addicts and alcoholics repeatedly urge the person in active addiction to 'do something' about himself or herself. And yet, an individual who has been accustomed to taking responsibility, to taking all the important decisions and generally making the running, while their partner was sick, may not like it much when that partner is suddenly 'back in the game'. When one of the partners in a relationship is sick, the relationship is, inevitably, sick. This is even more true when both are sick. It is to be hoped that, with recovery, the relationship will be healed. But sometimes the best 'healing' of a relationship, which was unsuitable in the first place, is its dissolution or 'redefinition'.

Another most compelling reason for avoiding any *new* sexual or romantic relationships in early recovery is that the problems associated with them contribute to a great many relapses. This should not surprise us. When we are in active addiction, our relationships are, of necessity, sick. But we remain sick, in many ways and for some time, even after we have become abstinent. As a result of working this programme we become more and more well. This takes time, however, and while we are still sick we are often attracted to other sick people. 'Sickness attracts sickness' runs one of the apophthegms often heard around the rooms of the Anonymous Fellowships. It is also true that sickness *reinforces* sickness. If I am in a relationship with another sick person, in early recovery, the probability is that we shall both get sicker. We like to persuade ourselves, of course, that we shall reinforce each others' *recovery* – that the relationship is mutually beneficial and that we are 'good for each other'. This is usually wishful thinking.

I don't suppose that the above considerations will dissuade a single addict in early recovery from embarking on a relationship, if that is what they have in mind. It did not stop me! We all like to believe that our relationship is *different*: that what may be true for others does not apply in our *special* case. That this is *real* love – and cannot be harmful. As a counsellor, I hear this kind of thing all the time. I have said such things myself. "You can't generalise. Surely, there must be exceptions?" etc. etc. The result was that I relapsed in the manner recounted in Chapter 6. And this is the usual outcome. Sooner or later, one or the other of the parties may find that they are not equipped to deal with the emotional implications of the new relationship - and relapse follows. Sometimes for both. Occasionally, alas, one or other of the parties may die as a result. We should not, therefore, enter lightly into such relationships in early recovery. Nor should we allow our recovery to become dependent on another person. If, for whatever reason, that person is no longer there, what happens to our recovery?

While these warnings may not prevent anyone from trying the experiment of getting involved in a 'relationship' in early recovery, it is to be hoped that they may, at least, persuade people not to repeat the experiment – if they are lucky enough to survive the first trial.

One final point on the subject of relationships. Nobody likes having to postpone the enjoyment of a proposed experience – least of all addicts! But of one thing we may be certain. If we *are* willing to wait until we are really well, any relationships we may have thereafter will be incomparably better than anything we have hitherto experienced. Healthy relationships are always preferable to sick ones. My wily sponsor deployed the suggestion that, until I had at least completed Step Eight to the best of my ability, I would do well to avoid any sexual or romantic relationships, as an incentive for me to attend to my Stepwork. Eventually, and up to a point, it worked. I was not to know that, by the time I had started upon Step Nine, I would no longer wish to rush into any of the kind of relationships which I had formerly proposed to myself so eagerly. I began to see that most of the relationships to which I had been accustomed were not very healthy. Crucially, I began to understand that what I could *give* to a relationship was much more important than what I could get out of it. My failure to grasp this any sooner had been part of the emotional immaturity which accompanied my active addiction.

It is often said that we addicts stop growing emotionally when we first pick-up mood altering substances or processes. It is certainly true that many of us seem to suffer from a kind of arrested emotional development. I did not enter fully upon my own emotional adolescence until the age of thirty-nine. To be almost forty years old, going on fourteen, is a strange, painful and bewildering experience. Fortunately, this Programme is, amongst other things, a crash-course in growing-up.

For these reasons, by the time we reach Step Eight, our eagerness to get on with our work on personal change (or perhaps our eagerness to get into a relationship!) is often tempered by an opposite inclination. Once we begin to understand the enormity of what is demanded by this Step, our over-enthusiastic haste may be moderated by a tendency towards procrastination. I certainly procrastinated long and assiduously over Step Eight - as soon as I began to understand what might be required of me. I even procrastinated as much as possible before writing this chapter on Step Eight! Nearly all my sponsees have likewise been smitten by inertia in the face of Steps Eight and Nine. Why should this be...? Well, in the first place, Steps Eight and Nine require us to revisit places we have been to in Steps Four and Five – uncomfortable places that we would rather avoid, if possible. In the second place, we are required by these Steps to change our attitudes to many past events and to many pivotal people. In the third place we know that we shall soon be required to take positive – and possibly difficult – action. Nevertheless, as we shall see in the **Actions** section which follows, we do not have to turn Steps Eight and Nine into another Big Deal.

Just as there are those who say that we should not enter into any new 'relationships' within some arbitrary period of time after becoming abstinent from our substances and processes of choice, so there are many who say that we should not make *any* major, life-changing decisions whatever, until we have been in recovery for at least one or two years. This is not quite as arbitrary as it may sound – but it is still rather arbitrary and can sometimes be impractical. It goes without saying that our capacity to make sane decisions will depend more on our progress in this programme than upon the mere passage of time. Nevertheless, there is much wisdom in the rule-of-thumb that, for every year that we have spent in active addiction, we shall need at least one month of 'clean-time' to restore some semblance of balance. Thus, if we were in active addiction for eighteen or twenty eight years we shall need at least eighteen or twenty eight months of recovery before we become reasonably stable and functional as human beings. It is sensible, during this period of readjustment, to discuss any unavoidable decision-making with our sponsor and with others in recovery.

In principle, however, we do not have to plod away for years before we reach Steps Eight and Nine. One sometimes hears, in one or other of the fellowships, of people who think that one Step per year is about right. It may be – for them. It should be remembered, however, that some of the original members of the earliest Fellowship were practising *all twelve* Steps within weeks or months of getting sober!

ACTIONS   *13.*

It is a principle of textual scholarship that, where two or more possible interpretations may be put upon a particular text, the most natural, obvious and literal is to be preferred. The text of the Eighth Step reads as follows:
Step Eight.
We made a list of all persons we had harmed, and became willing to make amends to them all.

*What does this Step conspicuously **not** say?*

It does not say that we made a mental note of the names of some of the people who might have been harmed by our behaviours and thought about maybe saying sorry sometime.

*It says **"We made a list"**... Our experience of previous Steps has taught us that, when the authors of the AA 'Big Book' talk about lists, examples or inventories, they generally have in mind something involving paper and writing. Much as we may squirm at the idea and try to wriggle out of it, we are going to have to put down the names of real people to whom we have done real harm. We are going to have to do this without making excuses for our actions, without trying to justify what we have done, without pretending that we can't really remember, without procrastinating and despite the fact that we may not like some of the people concerned - and even though some of these people may also have done us great harm. That is, at present, irrelevant.*

*Not only are we going to have to make this ghastly list, but we are also going to have to develop the **willingness** and intention to make a real and meaningful amend to each and every one of the people on our list. It will almost certainly turn out to be impossible or inappropriate to do so in some cases. But, at this point, we should not even consider such questions. We need to act as though we believe in the possibility of making the amend. In the due process of time, many amends, which we were convinced could never happen, **do** become possible. But, for now, we may (at the very least) be called on to learn to think kindly of people* *for whom we have hitherto felt only hatred. Remember, we do this for our own sakes. Hating people is not much fun.*

In some cases, where we genuinely do not know what the outcome of some of our past actions has been, it is incumbent upon us to do some active research. If we suspect that we may have harmed someone – but we are not certain – we need to find out: not just in order to consider an amend, but to stop the incident from preying on our mind.

(A routine example. Some years ago I was invited, by a friend whom I had known since childhood, to attend a steam-rally. I was drug-laden and drunk and behaving boorishly. My friend had an acquaintance, who owned a beautiful vintage motor-coach which had been converted into a travelling home. The owner of this unusual and exquisite coach-home decided that my intoxicated presence on board was not contributing to the general welfare and merriment of the party – and threw me off. I had a vague memory of taking my revenge by pissing in his fuel tank. But I was not sure if the memory was accurate. If it were true, it would almost certainly have wrecked his vintage and valued engine. Some years later, therefore, I needed to ask my friend about the facts and consequences of the incident, before I could consider the possibilities for making amends.)

Many people in recovery have committed serious crimes when they were in active addiction. For some, crime itself has been an addiction. Often an individual may know that he or she has committed a certain crime for which somebody else has been blamed – or for which nobody has ever been brought to justice. Should this be disclosed to anyone? Should any attempt be made to make an amend? Who else might be affected? These are delicate questions to which there is no single infallible answer. Each case must be addressed according to the circumstances - and after consultation with our sponsor. We shall consider such matters further in connection with Step Nine. What is important in the context of Step Eight is to admit honestly **to ourselves** *the harm which we have done to others and to be ready and willing to make amends, should the opportunity arise.*

As to the question of disclosure, it is to be hoped that these matters will already have been addressed, with at least **one** *other human being, in Steps Four and Five. If this is not the case, they should certainly be 'mopped up' in Step Ten. It is never a good idea for people who suffer from addictive disease to carry around guilty secrets. Sooner or later we use on them.*

Many of the names which belong on our Step Eight list will already have cropped up elsewhere – most notably in our Step Four work. But there will also be many new names on the list. This is partly because we are approaching the issue from a slightly different perspective. We are acknowledging more systematically the harm we have done, rather than examining it from the perspective of our resentments. But it is also because, as a result of Steps Six and Seven, we may be able to see more clearly where we have been at fault – and be more ready to admit it. Furthermore, in this Step we do not look only at the people who have been harmed while we were in active addiction. We need also to consider people whom we harmed before we ever 'picked up' (we will already have been exhibiting addictive characteristics) **and** those people whom we have harmed **since** we came into recovery. This Step has to do with the whole of our life, not just a limited section of it.

Let's use the familiar three-column schema to draw up our Step Eight list. In the first column, we shall write the names of the people whom we think we have harmed. Note that, where amends are concerned, we deal only with people – not with institutions and organisations. Amends are personal. This, presumably, is why Step Eight says that we made a list 'of all **persons** we had harmed…'. As with our Step Four schema, it is a good idea to do it in (roughly) reverse chronological order. We start with contemporary and recent events - and work backwards.

In the second column we shall write down, as concisely as possible, the harm which we have occasioned them.

To help us to become **willing** to make our amends - and to bring some sense of reality and immediacy to our intention - we shall set down in the third column some ideas for possible amends. In making amends, we should always strive to do something which helps to right the wrong which we have done. Usually this involves more than a simple apology. Nevertheless, the value of a sincere apology to the recipient should not be underestimated. Sometimes, nothing else is possible. We certainly should not allow misplaced pride to prevent us from making any apologies which are due.

If, at present, the possible nature of any amend is still unclear, we simply write DYK – Don't Yet Know. We shall, in any case be discussing our list and the proposed amends with our Sponsor, before any of the entries are finalised – and certainly before we attempt to start making any of our amends. Nevertheless, we should not overemploy DYK – nor use it as an excuse for mental laziness.

Let's see what our Step Eight list might begin to look like:

Whom did I harm?	**What** harm did I do?	**How** might I make amends?
Peter (at work).	Blamed him for the filing mistake.	Admit to boss that **I** made the mistake and apologise to Peter.
Amelia	Was instrumental in the break-up of her marriage.	Keep out of her present life altogether. Pray for her.
Jim (Amelia's husband).	Ditto.	Keep out of his present life. Acknowledge my wrong-doing if the occasion ever arises. Pray for him.
My step-father.	Stole his gold card case.	Admit it to him and gradually repay the money.
Old Maisie (now almost certainly dead).	Sold her a dud radio.	DYK. Possible symbolic amend. Contribution to **Age Concern**?
Etc.	Etc.	Etc.

Remember that the third column is not finalised. It contains only some preliminary ideas. Its main function is to help us to become **willing** to make amends. Later, as part of our work in connection with Step Nine, we shall be discussing with our Sponsor when and whether it is appropriate to make **direct** amends – and where it is not appropriate to do so.

There is also a sense in which our list of the people whom we have harmed is never completely finalised. We should finish it to the best of our current ability, and we should discuss it with our Sponsor. But, as time goes by, it is very likely that we shall remember other people who have been harmed by our actions, but who were not on our original list. We shall also probably begin to realise that people whom we did not think had been harmed by our behaviour, actually were – and should have been listed. Do not worry about this. Regular work on Step Ten will address these issues.

For now it is important to:

13. a.

Make your list along the lines indicated in the schema above.

13. b.

Take your list to your Sponsor and discuss it with him or her until you are sure that you have **become willing** to make these amends.

14.   RESTORING THE BALANCE – STEP NINE

Step Nine.
We made direct amends to such people wherever possible, except when to do so would injure them or others.

As one who has been actively involved in the 'therapy industry' for some years, I have good reason to know that it is an industry in which there often seems to be a multitude of people speaking a great deal of claptrap. It is an industry replete with pseudo-scientific jargon and with gobbledegook. And the volume of claptrap spoken in connection with the topic of 'self-esteem' is especially impressive. It is a subject which is in urgent need of demythologising.

For a start, I dislike the term 'self-esteem'. It seems to me to be much simpler and more concise to say that a person has a rather poor opinion of himself, than to say that he 'suffers from low self-esteem'. It is, in my view, simplistic and misleading to speak of 'self-esteem' as though it were a quantity which can be measured (perhaps by a special gauge) on a scale reading from Low to High. For most people, I suspect that there are certain things which they like about themselves – and there are certain things which they dislike about themselves. Fortunately, during the course of a lifetime, these things are subject to change. However, the term 'self-esteem' is now so ubiquitous that it has acquired a certain usefulness as shorthand and, with the above reservations, I shall continue to use it.

What is called 'self-esteem' has two principal sources. Some of our opinions about ourselves and about life are formed very early and have their origins in messages which we have received during childhood from others – usually significant adults, but sometimes siblings, peers and other contemporaries. These messages may be verbal or non-verbal. The ways in which we interpret rejection or abandonment, for instance, at any stage of life, may leave our 'self-esteem' somewhat dented. Verbal messages about ourselves, received when we are young, may include such articles of faith as "You're clumsy", "You're clever", "You're lazy", "You work hard", "You're fat and ugly", "You're handsome/pretty etc.". Messages about life may include such ideas as "Whatever you turn your hand to, you'll succeed", "You'll never amount to anything", "The world is your oyster", "Life is shit, and then you die", etc. Because, at this stage of life, our powers of discrimination are not fully formed, we may also absorb many apparently contradictory beliefs about ourselves - and accept them **all** as true.

One particularly pernicious belief about life which I absorbed at an early age was "Those who ask don't get; those who don't ask don't want". It leaves a child with nowhere to go! The clear message is "Whatever you do, you can't win".

If we have absorbed and internalised damaging beliefs about ourselves and about the world, it can take much hard work and a considerable period of time to begin to counteract these negative effects. This is one of the areas in which Cognitive Behaviour Therapy can be quite useful.

However, there is a second major source of our 'self-esteem' about which we *can* do something much more practical and much more immediate. Most addicts/alcoholics, when they first come into recovery, have a pretty poor opinion of themselves. Paradoxically, it may sometimes be accompanied by a huge and inflated ego (which is developed as a defensive countermeasure). But, at some level, we usually believe that we are 'bad' people. This is not surprising.

It is often assumed by the uninformed that people who suffer from addictive disease are deficient in the matter of conscience. If it were not so, how could we possibly go on doing things which damage and hurt the people closest to us? Sometimes, we almost manage to convince *ourselves* that we couldn't care less about other people; that we have no conscience and are only interested in 'looking after Number One'.

Wouldn't it be nice if that were true? It would make our lives so much simpler and easier to bear. But the truth is that there are probably no more conscience-free psychopaths and sociopaths among alcoholics and other addicts than there are, proportionately, in the population at large.

Actually, even when we are in active addiction, most of us have a perfectly serviceable set of principles and beliefs, ideas of good and bad, of right and wrong. The tragedy of addiction is not that we have no conscience. It is that that we are driven by our disease to do things (and to go on doing things) *which are completely contrary to our own most basic principles*, things which are in opposition to our own most deeply held beliefs. This has two main consequences:

1. We use/drink/act-out more and more, in an effort to blot out this guilty knowledge. This usually results in yet more shameful actions.

2. We end up feeling pretty lousy about ourselves. We end up with a very low opinion of ourselves. We end up, if you will, 'suffering from low self-esteem'.

There is an aspect of our compulsive nature which I call 'obduracy in wrongdoing'. I don't suppose that it is the exclusive preserve of addicts and alcoholics – but it does seem to be a characteristic to which we are peculiarly prone. In a nutshell, it is this. We know that a particular course of action is wrong. We know that it will not help us – or anybody else. But we obstinately pursue this course of action, as if we wish to demonstrate to ourselves and to others that there is nothing wrong with it, that it is perfectly normal and that we have been right, all along, to keep on doing it.

One of the most familiar examples of this, at least to counsellors who work in treatment centres, is the patient who returns from a relapse precipitated by an unsuitable 'relationship', who swears that he or she has learned the obvious lesson, that relationships are now the last thing on his/her mind, that he/she already has a partner at home and wants to concentrate solely on recovery but who, nevertheless, within a few days of readmission is seen to have embarked upon yet another 'exclusive relationship'.

When our observable behaviours are directly contrary to our consciously formulated intentions, it is usually a very strong indication that an addictive process is at work.

In active addiction, this 'obduracy in wrongdoing' may take many different forms. It may involve repeated and unnecessary criminal acts: car-thefts, muggings, burglaries, violence etc. It may involve sexual behaviours of which we are ashamed. It usually involves mood-altering processes over which, during active addiction, we seem to lack the power of choice. But the acknowledged underlying rationale for this obdurate persistence is also, in part, the same. By repeating the behaviour, we hope, somehow, to 'normalise' it.

We never achieve this, of course. We simply end up feeling worse and worse about ourselves. Our rock-bottom 'self-esteem' falls right through the rock-floor.

What can be done?

There is a school of thought among some counsellors and 'therapists' that people with 'low self-esteem' should be advised to do 'mirror work'. This means that you are supposed to gaze lovingly at your own reflection in a mirror and repeat endlessly that you are a wonderful, gifted, intelligent, beautiful, talented and *worthwhile* person. You are meant to tell your reflection how much you *love* yourself. Although there is a place for certain types of mirror-work in the treatment of individuals with body-image problems as a result of eating disorders, as a general treatment for low self-esteem, mirror-work is wholly inappropriate. You may end up with an even more inflated ego as a result of this type of 'therapy' - but your underlying opinion of yourself (your 'self-esteem') is unlikely to improve very much. Nor, as a result of it, will you become any more wonderful, gifted, intelligent or beautiful than you already are. You may, in the fullness of time and for completely different reasons, become all of these things – but it is improbable that it will happen as a result of 'mirror work'.

Fortunately the solution to this problem is not, as they say nowadays, 'rocket science'. In fact, it is astonishingly simple.

First, we become abstinent from our addictive substances and processes.

Then, in recovery, WE STOP DOING THE THINGS THAT MAKE US FEEL BAD ABOUT OURSELVES – AND WE START DOING SOME THINGS THAT MAKE US FEEL GOOD ABOUT OURSELVES.

In other words, we start to practise this programme of recovery. And, of all the Steps in this 12-Step programme of recovery, it is this one, Step Nine, which has the most salutary effect upon our 'self-esteem'.

Naturally, we embark upon Step Nine, first and foremost, to set right the wrongs that we have done to others - to redress, in some small measure, their pain. But we do it, too, to begin to build ourselves into the kind of people we would like to be – individuals of whom we can approve. As long as we go on *disliking* ourselves, not only will our relationships with others be complex and unrewarding, but we run the risk of seeking our usual escape from our uncomfortable feelings – the risk of 'picking up'. *Telling* our reflection in a mirror how much we like ourselves will not work. *Doing* things that make us feel better about ourselves will. And, gradually, as time goes by and our accomplishments begin to accumulate, we *do* begin to feel better about ourselves.

Remember, we are not *bad* people trying to get *good*. We have been very *sick* people – and we are trying to get *well*. We are gradually becoming the sort of people we should have been - if our lives had not been temporarily diverted by this abominable disease.

In Step Ten, we shall ask ourselves what kind of people we *would* like to be. For now, however, let's take some more positive *actions*.

ACTIONS   14.

14. a.

*Take your Amends List (agreed with your sponsor in Step Eight) and decide which of the proposed amends is, from a **practical** point of view, the most **difficult** to make.*

This may be, for instance, because you don't know what has happened to a friend from whom you stole something or because you don't yet have the means to make the appropriate amend.

***Do something today** which sets the process in motion and brings you closer to the point where you can make the amend. For example, research the person's current whereabouts through contacts or on the internet. Do something which will help you to replace what was stolen.*

This is merely one of many possible examples. Each person's case will be different.

14. b.

*Look again at the Amends List agreed with your sponsor in Step Eight and decide which of the proposed amends is, from a **practical** point of view, the **easiest** to make. This may be because the person concerned lives next door and you now have the means to repay the money you borrowed three years ago – or it may be for other practical reasons. Whatever the case and whatever the amend may be, if it is fairly easy and practicable, do it NOW! **Today.***

14. c.

Repeat actions 14. a. and 14. b. every day until you have crossed off all the names on your list. This may take rather a long time – and some of them may prove to be impossible (for the foreseeable future). We are aiming, remember, for progress – not for perfection. However, as you take small, achievable measures towards accomplishing the more difficult amends, they will begin to seem less hard - and their positions on your list will change. If you encounter any great difficulties, consult your sponsor.

You may well find that there are occasions when your effort to make an amend is not greatly appreciated or welcomed by the intended recipient. They may tell you to fuck off. That's OK. You have done your part. As the AA 'Big Book' says; you can only clean up your side of the street.

15. TENDING THE GARDEN – STEP TEN

Steps 10, 11 and 12 (the last three Steps of this recovery programme) are sometimes called 'the maintenance Steps'. The idea underlying this usage is that, having achieved some measure of health by means of the preceding Steps, we need now to 'maintain' our recovery with the remaining three Steps. There is nothing much wrong with this idea – provided we do not allow it to lead us into complacency. We cannot afford to stop practising the principles of the nine previous Steps, in the hope that the 'maintenance' Steps alone will sustain us.

They won't.

I may continue to take personal inventory (Step 10). I may pray and I may meditate (Step 11). I may try to carry the message as a result of my spiritual awakening (Step 12). But if I forget that I am powerless over my addiction (Step 1), I'm sunk.

One of the main purposes of Step Ten (and of all the other Steps) is what is sometimes called 'relapse prevention'. In one of the rehabs where I worked as a counsellor, each client was at one time given an impressive-looking personal 'Relapse Prevention Plan'. It was devoted mainly to avoiding situations in which the individual might use alcohol or other drugs excessively. The intention behind such an exercise is admirable. But it exhibits a deplorable ignorance of the nature and characteristics of addictive disease. With my own patients, I like to use a slightly different approach, which I learned from Dr Robert Lefever. We work out, together, a Continuing Recovery Plan.

This difference in emphasis is important. If someone who has been in recovery starts using mood-altering substances or processes again, he or she is often said to have 'relapsed'. But getting the alcohol or other drug into our bodies is not a relapse. It is only *a sign that we are already in a state of relapse*. The state of relapse is the opposite of the state of remission. But, because this state does not arise suddenly and without warning, relapse is also a process.

If I am spiritually well, I instinctively avoid mood-altering substances and processes. It is only when I become spiritually sick - when the insanity returns - that using drugs (like alcohol or heroin) or using other addictive processes (bingeing, starving, sex, gambling, etc.) begins to look like a sensible and attractive plan. The relapse process starts long before we pick up a drink, drug or other addictive process. Relapse is not the act of picking up. It is the state of mind which permits us to pick up.

If a diabetic neglects to take his insulin each day, he becomes sick. Similarly, if I neglect to do the things which I need to do to maintain my recovery, I will become sick. There are certain things which I need to do *every day* in order to remain in a state of remission from my disease. If I cease to do these things, I will become miserable and will fall into a state of relapse. If I fall into a state of relapse, it is very probable that I shall start using alcohol or other addictive substances and behaviours again. That, at any rate, is what always used to happen in the past! And that way death and madness lie.

It is also possible to be in a state of full relapse *without* picking up a drink or other drug. This phenomenon has been recognised since the earliest days of recovery. To the early AAs it was known as the 'dry drunk'. Shortly after I got abstinent from drink and drugs, my first Sponsor sometimes used to introduce me to old-timers in the Fellowship. "This is John" he would say "He's not drinking or drugging – but he might as well be!" I was abstinent alright. But I was still barking mad. The old-timers would nod their heads sympathetically.

Nowadays, one of the things that I need to do on a daily basis to remain in a healthy condition is Step Ten. We shall be looking at some of the other things which are helpful for continuing recovery in a subsequent chapter. But, for now, let's look at what Step Ten actually says:

Step Ten.

We continued to take personal inventory and when we were wrong promptly admitted it.

Step Ten may be regarded as a means of preventing an accumulation of the kind of moral and emotional clutter which kept us sick in the past. By means of Steps 4 to 9 we have 'cleaned house'. We have brought fresh air and sunshine into the darker corners of our soul. Now we need to keep our soul's dwelling-place clear of any further dark detritus.

In the title to this chapter, I have used a horticultural metaphor. Any gardener will tell you that two of the most important operations in tending a garden are the weeding and the pruning. We need to weed out the plants which have no place in our garden - to prevent them from proliferating and taking over the whole garden. Sometimes we need to cut back even the useful and ornamental plants to prevent them from becoming unruly and excessive. Remember that addictive disease is capable of using even our *good* qualities against us. We shall look at some of the specific techniques for keeping our garden healthy in the *'Actions'* section of this chapter.

In previous chapters we have noted that Step Ten can also be very useful for 'mopping up' any material which we have inadvertently overlooked in Steps Five or Eight. It is not uncommon for people to realise, after they have completed Step Five, that, without consciously intending to, they have omitted some important material from their inventory. No big deal. Simply discuss the matter with your sponsor or some other suitable person as soon as you *do* remember it – and, if the person or persons affected by your behaviour also belong on your Step Eight list, take whatever action may be necessary or possible to redress the situation.

It is important to bear in mind that we do all these things, not because we are aiming at sainthood and wish to be perfect, nor because we are now reformed and wish to be 'goody-two-shoes', nor even because we think that such spiritual exercises will be of benefit to us and will improve us. We do all this because we don't want to return to active addiction and because we would rather not die just yet.

ACTIONS 15.

Most people find that Step Ten work is best done towards the end of each day.

15. a.

Go over in your mind the events of the day, the people you have met, the things you have done or left undone, any conflicts that have arisen. In each case we need to ask ourselves the following questions:
Were my actions prompted by:

- *Fear?*
- *Resentment?*
- *Self-pity?*
- *Greed?*
- *Selfishness?*
- *Misplaced pride (hubris)?*
- *Need for power and control?*
- *Promoting my own comfort, convenience or advantage at the expense of others?*

*We need not be (and we should not be) **over**scrupulous in enumerating our faults and delinquencies. That, in itself, can be a form of spiritual pride. It may also leave us feeling so rotten about ourselves that we are of little use to others. Addictive disease likes it when we feel rotten about ourselves. We are more likely to 'use'.*

15. b.

*Decide what, if anything, should be done about the above incidents. Have other people been harmed by my actions today? What amends can I make tomorrow? To whom should I admit that I was wrong? **Make a list of specific measures which you can take.** If any of them can be done straight away, either in person or on the telephone, **do them.** Otherwise, write them down on your list of actions for the following day. It is a good* idea to keep a permanent 'Action Book' (you can use a diary or even an electronic PDA). You can thus keep track of your intentions and cross off those which have been completed.

15. c.

If you are in doubt about any of the matters which you have considered – and the hour is not too late – **phone your sponsor**. (Leave this till the following morning if you keep uncivilised hours!)

15. d.

If you have remembered any material from the more distant past which was not included in your Step Four inventory or on your Step Eight list, make a note of it and discuss it with your sponsor at the earliest opportunity.

15. e.

Repeat the above actions, every evening.

16. NOURISHING THE GARDEN – STEP ELEVEN

We have already had occasion to say something about prayer. People pray for all kinds of different reasons. But, for anyone who suffers from addictive disease, the most compelling reason for adopting this practice is that, over the decades since the pioneers of recovery first started to work this programme, hundreds of thousands of people have noticed that prayer helps them to achieve and sustain a healthy, happy and productive recovery. And it is observable, around the fellowships, that many of those who seem most sane - and who appear to enjoy life the most - are advocates of this practice.

I have been extremely lucky.

One day, when I was drunk in Plaistow, I blundered into the presence of God.

Now, many are at liberty to say (and doubtless will say) that this was a delusion brought on by intoxication. I cannot prove that they are wrong. However, there have been a couple of occasions, since I came into recovery, when I have felt again God's presence in a similar and overwhelming way.

The mechanists, of course, will say that this is merely my interpretation of some subjective sensations which may be accounted for by the malfunctioning of my neurological systems and by long-term drug-damage to the bio-electrical and chemical activities of my brain. A mild form of epilepsy, perhaps – or possibly a 'mini' stroke. Or maybe just another problem arising from my addictive, neurotransmission disease.

Again, I cannot prove them wrong. Nor do I wish to waste my time in the attempt. What I do know, however, is that, when it first happened in Plaistow, the experience sobered me up completely and immediately – and no matter how much alcohol I drank in the ensuing days, I found it impossible to get drunk.

At the time when it happened, I had already grown out of my rebellious, adolescent atheism. So, again, it may be thought that the experience was some kind of unconscious fulfilment of my expectations. I can only say that it did not correspond in any way to any of my preconceived ideas of a 'theophany'! It was actually a rather terrifying experience.

It is very difficult to describe.

I did not see visions and I did not hear any voices. I felt as though I had been engulfed in an incredibly powerful energy-field. Then I sensed, rather than saw, that a gap seemed to have opened up in the space-time continuum somewhere 'above' my head. And in this 'gap' inconceivable forces were at work – forces by comparison with which everything in my previous experience disappeared into insignificance. I felt that all my puny human knowledge amounted to nothing.

Up to this point in my life, I had taken a rather cynical and jaundiced view of the world and of everything in it. Indeed many of my friends today still regard me as an incorrigible sceptic. I am certainly not known as someone who is much given to 'awe'. But on this occasion – and on two subsequent occasions – it was certainly awe that I felt.

Whether these experiences were merely 'tricks of the mind', I do not now know or care. To me it did not seem so at the time. I remember wondering vaguely how I would explain all this to myself later; how I could rationalise it all away. Would I be able to deny to myself that anything significant had happened? I have tried very hard to do so. But, at the root of my being, I am left with a single abiding consequence. It is not a belief nor even a conviction. It is a *knowledge* that there is a Power greater than myself - a power far beyond my poor, limited, human understanding. A power that I call God.

That is why I consider myself lucky.

The immediate salutary effects of these experiences did not last more than a couple of weeks. Nor were they, in themselves, enough to deal with my addictive disorders. It was not until I had learned, in treatment, how to begin to apply the principles of this programme of recovery that there was any perceptible effect upon my addictive disease. I do not even regard these experiences as having constituted any kind of 'spiritual awakening'. I experienced a rude awakening, certainly. But that is not quite the same thing as the 'spiritual awakening' referred to in Step Twelve.

It should not be supposed, moreover, that experiences of this kind are *necessary* to recovery. They seem to be the exception rather than the rule. Nevertheless, during the course of my work as an addictions counsellor, I have been surprised at the number of people who *have* reported 'paranormal' experiences of one sort or another. Personally, I have far greater admiration for the great majority of people in recovery, whose recovery rests more on trust and on faith than on these kinds of experience.

Step Eleven reads as follows:

Step Eleven.
We sought through prayer and meditation to improve our conscious contact with God *as we understood Him*, praying only for knowledge of His will for us and the power to carry that out.

I have indicated above that I do not consider it possible for me, a mere mortal, fully to understand God. I cannot even, with any confidence, use the pronoun 'He' in connection with God – rather than 'She' or 'It'. But this does not mean that I should not seek to understand something of God's nature and what bearing, if any, that might have on my life and on the way in which I conduct it.

At the same time, however, it would be presumptuous of me to suggest to anyone else how they should approach the practices of prayer and meditation. If you have borne with me up to this point, it is very likely that you will already have formed your own ideas about God and about your means of 'improving' your 'conscious contact' with God.

The remarks which follow, therefore, should not be regarded as prescriptive. They are included merely to extend an interesting discussion. In Appendix II, at the end of this book, I shall record some suggestions which my first sponsor made to me in this connection – and which I have found to be extremely helpful. But, for now, let's return to our sources. Let's try to see what the authors of the AA 'Big Book' had in mind.

The first thing which is clear is that the originators of this programme no longer even troubled themselves with the question of whether or not there was a God. They took it for granted that there was. That was their experience - and they were unable to account in any other way for their apparently miraculous recoveries.

Of course it *is* possible to account for these apparent 'miracles' in other ways. Perhaps it was merely auto-suggestion. Perhaps their misplaced faith in their own deluded ideas about divine intervention was so strong that it produced the effect for which they had hoped. It is always possible to rationalise, to discount, to reduce. But let us pretend, for a moment and simply for the sake of argument, that their central tenet is correct: that there is a God whose help may be sought and who intervenes in the lives of 'incurable' addicts and alcoholics to relieve them of the of their compulsion to 'use'. What follows?

What seems to follow, according to the 'Big Book', is that we have a duty to *communicate* with God. We do this through *prayer and meditation*. And this communication has one purpose and one purpose only. We are seeking knowledge of God's will for us – and the ability to perform it.

As has been said before, this is an intensely *practical* programme of recovery. It does not concern itself with philosophical and theological speculations on the existence and nature of God. It is a programme of *actions* and *decisions*. It suggests, on the basis of experience, what we can *do* to be free of addiction – in fact, to save our lives.

During my first treatment in Wiltshire (long before my experience in Plaistow), I wanted to argue the toss about the existence or non-existence of God. It saved me the trouble of *doing* anything about my condition. The same counsellor whom I had exasperated with my complaints about the 'dehumanising' regime in the treatment centre became equally frustrated with the theological and philosophical niceties which I was expounding. Finally he turned to me and said "Listen, John. Do you want to be right? Or do you want to *live*?" It was a close call at the time! But I decided that, on balance, I would prefer to live. I would rather be a clean, sober, healthy and contented believer than a dead atheist.

Precisely *how*, then, do the authors of the AA 'Big Book' suggest that we might enter into communication with our Higher Power? Let us return to Step Eleven. Let's try to discover the intentions of its authors in respect of prayer and meditation.

By the word 'meditation', they do *not* seem to mean the kind of practice which had its origins in the East and became fashionable in the West from the late 1960s onwards. At the time when the Big Book was written, nobody in the West had heard of 'Transcendental Meditation'. It is unlikely that either Bill W. or Dr Bob were familiar with any of the more esoteric oriental schools of meditation. These practices may, indeed, be extremely helpful to some people. But it is unlikely that they are what the originators of this Programme had in mind.

Many years ago, long before I was given an effective means of dealing with my addictive disorders and in an effort to limit the damage caused by my addictive disease, I took refuge in a monastic community. I lived there for more than a year, naïvely hoping that, confined within the cloister, I would be unable to do much further harm – to myself or to the world. It was an unusual place.

It was run by a rather eccentric monk belonging to one of the Anglican monastic orders. They had found it difficult to decide what to do with him. They sent him, therefore, to India for thirteen years. When he returned, they still didn't know what to do with him. So they gave him a house and some land in Sussex – and allowed him to start a kind of '*ashram*' there. He assembled around himself a small community and attempted to combine the meditative and yogic techniques which he had learned in the East with the Western Christian contemplative tradition - with, it must be admitted, rather peculiar results.

In this community, we kept the traditional daily 'offices' of Prime, Mattins (Morning Prayer), Terce, Sext, None, Vespers (Evensong) and Compline - though in some cases they were combined together. But, instead of gathering together in the customary rows and pews of a conventional chapel, we all sat cross-legged (in the Lotus posture) in the little sanctum which was used for this purpose. Mattins and Vespers were accompanied by lengthy periods of meditation.

During these meditations I sat there dutifully, like the rest. I grew accustomed to the physical discomfort and was able to disregard it. I attempted to still my mind – to stop the 'internal dialogue' and to become one with God. I felt, on many occasions, that I was succeeding. I even imagined that we were in telepathic communication with one another and that we were radiating 'positive energy' into the world.

At mid-morning, in a spacious annexe, we all participated in what was called a 'meditation of movement'. This consisted of adopting a series of different yogic postures (*asanas*), doing some T'ai Chi (of which I could never get the hang) and a very slow 'meditation walk' around the room. During the rest of the day we worked on the land, looked after the goats and attended to domestic chores. Even these, however, were regarded as 'contemplative' activities. You did not simply *do* the cooking or *do* the washing-up. You performed a 'meditation of cooking' or a 'meditation of washing-up'.

I do not want to make all this sound too bizarre and laughable – because I think that, in fact, there is much to be said for a way of life which gives due consideration to every daily activity. And I think that, in the long term, my stay in this little community and the 'regular' life did me much good. But it did not solve the problem of my addictive disease.

It was not long before I discovered that, by clambering over a wall at night, I could get to the local pub. On the first occasion, I drank only one pint of beer and I made it last a whole hour. Then I climbed back over the wall and went to bed.

I slept soundly and awoke the next morning feeling clear-headed, alert and refreshed. The early sun was shining. The birds were singing. Spring buds were opening on the greening trees. The sky had not fallen. The abyss had not opened up beneath my feet. I went about my daily tasks with a spring in my step. I felt no imperative need to go and have another drink or to start taking other drugs. Indeed, I did not repeat the experiment for another fortnight.

But one of the most dangerous thoughts which can possibly occur to an addict or alcoholic had already entered my head.

This is the thought:

"Got away with it!"

After a fortnight I repeated the experiment. Again, it was a resounding success. I drank only two pints – and I made them last two hours. I clambered back over the wall. I went to sleep. I got up in the morning. I did what was required of me. I had got away with it. Again!

Somehow or other, though, several months down the line, I got thrown out of the *ashram*. It was on the occasion when I had been arrested by the local police for attempting to carry off an enormous bottle of vintage port from a local wine-merchant - declaring that I was William Wilberforce and had come to free the slaves. I ended up in the local lunatic asylum.

It was where I belonged.

The reason why the thought "Got away with it!" is so dangerous for people like us is that it is often followed by another, equally dangerous, thought "Perhaps I'm normal, after all." We never get away with it. Normal people do. But we are not 'normal' – at least not in this sense. Even if nobody else ever knows that we have broken our abstinence, *we* know. And this knowledge may lead us to 'use' again.

Leading the 'religious' life of prayer and meditation plainly had not solved my problem.

If people who are in recovery wish to return to the religion in which they were raised, it is often a very helpful and productive course of action. Nevertheless, if religion alone were an adequate treatment for addictive disease, there would not be so many drunken priests. Religion, it is sometimes said, is for people who do not want to go to hell. Spirituality, on the other hand, which is the basis of this programme, is for people who have already been there. So, what kind of prayer and meditation *are* advocated by the 'Big Book' for the Eleventh Step?

ACTIONS   *16.*

*'On awakening' says the Big Book on p. 86, in reference to Step 11, 'let us think about the twenty-four hours ahead...' There follow some fairly detailed suggestions as to **how** we might think about the day to come. For example '...we ask God to direct our thinking'.*

'We usually conclude the period of meditation' it continues on p. 87 'with a prayer that we be shown all through the day what our next step is to be, that we be given whatever we need to take care of such problems'.

I cannot improve upon these suggestions from the Founding Fathers – and would not presume to try. Therefore...

16. a.

Turn to the bottom of p. 85 in the AA Big Book – and read through to the end of the chapter, on p. 88.

16. b.

*For those who are interested in further ideas for prayer and meditation, some suggestions (drawn from the experience of many fellowship members over many decades) are to be found in the next chapter and in **Appendix II, 'Seven Things Daily'** at the end of this book.*

17. HARVEST TIME – STEP TWELVE

This is the Twelfth Step:

Step Twelve.

Having had a spiritual awakening as the result of these steps, we tried to carry this message to those still in active addiction, and to practice these principles in all our affairs.

I consider myself to have been extremely fortunate. If my addictive disease had been allowed to run its course unchecked by this Programme, I would certainly be dead by now. I am living on borrowed time.

I have lost count of the former colleagues, former patients, relatives and close friends whom I have lost to this horrible illness - and I am conscious that it could still claim me.

This does not mean, however, that I have to live in an anxious state of perpetual vigilance. That would not be much fun. There are certain things which I need to do every day to avoid falling into a state of relapse. These things are not particularly onerous and they are not extraordinarily complicated. Nevertheless, it is not always easy for me to do them. Much repetition has now made many of them 'second nature' to me. But that term is the clue to the difficulty. They are part of my *second* nature. They are not my *first* nature. My first nature was from birth, is now, and will remain **addictive**.

There **is** such a thing as an addictive personality and, like millions of others, I've got it. It is probably caused by an inherited dysfunction in the neurotransmission systems. Therefore, most of the things which I need to do on a daily basis to remain sane and to continue growing in recovery do not come naturally to me. They are, if anything, quite contrary to all my natural inclinations. The measures which follow in the *Actions* section of this chapter were suggested to me by my first Sponsor, who had them from his Sponsor, who received them from his Sponsor… and so on back. They are actually nothing more than a simple way of 'practising these principles in all our affairs'.

"If you do these things," said my sponsor "you will not only get well and stay well, you might even get *happy*."

This seemed totally inconceivable to me. Unrelieved misery had become my habitual state. I had forgotten what it felt like to be happy. I was now grimly determined to remain *abstinent* for various practical reasons. But I *knew* that abstinence was a terrible ordeal – a sacrifice which would certainly intensify my misery. I had tried it before – and had found it unendurable. Yet here was this man, who claimed to have been in an equally dark and despondent condition, smilingly saying to me "Misery is optional"! It was infuriating. The man was clearly a lunatic. The 'happy-clappers' must have addled his wits.

Sensing my incredulity and irritation he said "I'll tell you what, John. Try it for thirty days. If you don't feel better after thirty days, you can come back and call me a *#*!*. Just try it. It can't do you any harm." Strange, I thought, '*#*!*' is not happy-clapper language.

I have never had to call this man a *#*!*.

I have called him many other names for all kinds of different reasons. But never for this reason. Because what he said was absolutely true. At the end of thirty days, not only had the compulsion to use/drink/etc. been lifted, but so, inexplicably, had my mood. I was actually beginning to enjoy life. Abstinence no longer seemed like a sacrifice and a grim daily struggle. My material circumstances had not improved at all. I was still living in a B & B in the East End. I was having to walk miles to Meetings because I could not afford public transport. But I had new friends and a new interest in life. Sometimes, more experienced members of the Fellowship were kind enough to take me with them on Twelfth Step calls to people who needed help.

At the end of thirty days, rather abashedly, I reported these favourable findings to my Sponsor.

"Try it for another sixty days." he said "It gets better!"

Unfortunately, on this occasion, I did not complete a further sixty days. Instead I gradually dropped my daily routine. I saved up some money and got on a train to a South Coast town - to 'carry the message' to a few old acquaintances who were still in active addiction. Regardless of my inexperience, I planned to show them how well I was and to help them to get clean and sober. I met them in a pub. We all got drunk together. Then they jumped me in the car park. They gave me a good kicking and stole what remained of my money. Poor bastards! They were very sick.

But so, for quite a long time after this, was I.

This illustrates the difficulty. I had been trying to run before I could walk. As long as I continued to do the things which my Sponsor suggested, all went well. But, if I followed my own inclinations and decided impulsively to start doing it my own way again, catastrophe seemed to ensue.

On a conscious level, I had fully intended to help my chums. But my addictive disease had other plans. It set me up. By using two of my defects (arrogance and the desire to show them how well I was doing) and one of my assets (my concern for others) it got me into a pub - where I had no business in early recovery. The rest was easy.

I limped back to London. I stopped going to Meetings altogether and soon started using drugs again. Many months later, when I had finally got back to the Fellowship and had reestablished contact with my sponsor, I told him this sorry tale.

"That" said he "is why I suggested to you that you should always go with another person who is in good recovery when you're trying to do Twelfth Step work." It is a principle which I still observe to this day. It is never a good idea to go on a Twelfth Step call alone. Nor is it a good idea to try to run before you have learned to walk.

Many people get very excited by the phrase 'spiritual awakening'. They conceive of it as a sudden, overwhelming event. They doggedly work their Steps with greater and greater vigour, in breathless anticipation. "When is it going to happen?" they wonder. When nothing spectacular does seem to happen, they revisit their Stepwork again and again, hoping to find some crucial ingredient which has been omitted from the recipe. 'Perhaps I did not fully admit my own powerlessness and unmanageability' they think. 'Maybe my faith is not strong enough', 'Have I *really* turned over my will and my life?' they wonder. 'Perhaps I was not searching and fearless enough.' 'Was I completely ready and willing?' 'Perhaps I was not humble enough.' If we are thinking along these lines, it is usually because we 'can't see the wood for the trees'. Let's look again at what Step Twelve actually says. **'Having had a spiritual awakening as the result of these steps...'** Note the past tense. By the time we reach Step Twelve, *it has already happened*. We were just too busy to notice.

There is another respect in which I consider that I have been very lucky. I have the privilege of working, every day, with people who are striving for recovery. But this is my professional work. I do not regard it as Twelfth Step work – and working in a treatment centre is certainly not a substitute for getting to meetings.

There are two questions which I sometimes put to the patients in the treatment centre. The first is "What kind of people were we when we were in active addiction?" Their answers are interesting. All kinds of adjectives are proposed – most of them not very complimentary. Devious. Lazy. Isolated. Dishonest. Selfish. Wasteful. Self-centred. Slippery. Violent. Chaotic. Uncaring. Cruel. Hard. Mercenary. Parasitic. The list continues to grow.

Then I ask them "What kind of people would we like to become, in recovery?" A different flock of adjectives fills the air. Caring. Honest. Trustworthy. Hard-working. Productive. Positive. Fair. Self-reliant. Gregarious. Team-players. Helpful. Loving. Fulfilled. Open. Happy. Surprisingly few people say 'rich', 'important' or 'powerful'. Then I point out that there is a huge gulf between the kind of people we have been - and the kind of people we would like to be. How can it be crossed?

The Twelve Step programme has often been called 'a bridge to normal living'. It is certainly that. But for most of us, it has been infinitely more than that. It has been a bridge across the gulf which separates the subhuman creatures which addiction made of us from the functioning, fulfilled, creative and contented human beings that we had always hoped to be. Now, at last, we begin to realise that we have somehow been crossing that bridge. We now have loved ones and friends. Our actions are in keeping with our values and beliefs. We are able to contribute to the world. Daily, we are given strength to meet our difficulties with steadiness and equanimity. Where once we saw only insurmountable problems we now see solutions and opportunities. Instead of living with fear and despair, we now live with courage, with faith, with hope, with gratitude and with peace. We live in the presence of our Higher Power. We may even, on occasion, feel the freedom, happiness and joy mentioned in the 'Big Book'. It seems to me to be no exaggeration to say that we have experienced a spiritual awakening!

ACTIONS   17.

Seven Things Daily

*These suggestions were made to me by my first sponsor. He had received them from his sponsor, who had received them from his sponsor etc. They are based, therefore, on the experience of several generations of people in recovery. They are to be found in abbreviated form in **Appendix II** – **Seven Things Daily**.*

They will not suit everybody – and each person is free to adapt them to his or her own individual needs.

As far as I know, they do not form part of any of the official literature of any of the Fellowships. Their appearance here is in no way prescriptive. I record them simply as a matter of historical interest. I will, however, add that, so far, they have worked for me – as long as I have continued to practise them. My adherence to them has never been perfect – and probably never will be. That is not the point. I have come to regard them as a simple way of practising the principles of the Twelve Step programme in my daily life. The more conscientious I am in the performance of these suggestions, the better they seem to work.

*What do I mean by 'work'? I mean quite simply that when I do these things, my life is happier, less convoluted, more productive, more effective than when I neglect to do them or when I do them only in a slipshod and half-hearted manner. I personally do not know anyone who has ever relapsed while actively following these suggestions. I do, however, know of people who have gradually **stopped** doing these things - and have returned for a while to active addiction. I was one of them.*

When I first heard these suggestions, I was extremely sceptical. I had gone round to my sponsor's flat one winter's afternoon because, although I was no longer using drugs or drinking, and although I had been working my programme, with my sponsors's help, up to Step Seven (to the best of my ability), I still felt restless and discontented.

"The first thing you need each day", said my Sponsor, "is a period of prayer and meditation. Every morning, as soon as you wake up", he continued, "roll out of bed – and onto your knees. Thank your Higher Power for another day in recovery and ask for help to stay clean and

sober for this one day." This was the best advice I received as a struggling newcomer.

In this one action, I am renewing the first three Steps of the recovery programme. I am admitting that I, personally, am powerless over my addictive disease (Step One). I am demonstrating my belief in the possibility of healing and restoration by a Higher Power (Step Two). In thus asking for help, I am turning over my will and my life to the care of that Higher Power (Step Three).

"Next", continued my Sponsor, "say your Third Step Prayer." I knew what he meant. He had asked me, as part of my work on Step Three, to write out, in my own words, the Third Step Prayer to be found on p. 63 of the AA 'Big Book'. I made a note of his suggestion.

*"Then, read your **Just for Today** card."*

This is a little card, to be found at any AA Meeting, which begins 'Just for today, I will try to live through this day only...' It is not to be confused with the admirable but more substantial book of daily meditations published under the same name by NA. My sponsor said that I should try to do everything on this little card during the course of the coming day. I have found that one of the great advantages of following this suggestion is that, nowadays, I seldom get bored. On this one little card, there is enough to keep me fully occupied for the greater part of each day!

Next, he said that I should write a Gratitude List. He explained that this consists of a list of things for which I am grateful, on this day. In the early days of my own recovery my list included such things as a roof over my head, a bed and at least one good meal the previous day. These were luxuries which I had not known for a long time. The list still includes the surprising facts that I am still alive and have most of my limbs and faculties. It is a very good way to start any day, because it generates a positive frame of mind.

My sponsor's next suggestion seemed very odd to me. "If you know that you are harbouring any anger or resentments against people," he said, "pray for the bastards. They're probably sick in some way, too." He explained that we should not pray that they would be seized by the Four Horsemen of the Apocolypse and tormented forever in the Inferno. We should pray for their well-being, happiness and peace. We should wish them all good things. "It is very hard", he said, "to do this – and mean it. But persevere for several days and, if necessary, for weeks. It is the surest way to rid ourselves of resentments. And it works both for people with whom we are currently angry and for the monsters of the past." I have found his words to be true.

To close this quiet time set aside first thing each morning, he suggested that I should add any prayers and meditations of my own choice.

He went on to say that, secondly, it was a good idea, at least in early recovery, to phone (or meet) our sponsor at some point during the course of the day and, thirdly, to get to a Meeting. He pointed out that, even though this latter may be difficult, we need to be prepared to go to the same lengths in pursuit of our recovery as once we did to sustain our addiction. Those who live in big cities should not have much difficulty with this. I used to walk miles through the East End of London to get to Meetings in places between Whitechapel and Ilford. I did not have the bus fare. In most big cities there are meetings to be found on any day of the week – and at many different times of day. Those who live in remote areas without public transport may not be able to get to meetings quite so easily. It is enough to make our best efforts. Or, for the sake of our recovery, we might consider moving.

My sponsor then suggested that every day, either at a meeting, or in a social context, or on the phone, it is a good idea to try to help a newcomer in some way. This help may be something simple (like offering them a cup of tea at a meeting to make them feel at home) or it could be spending time talking with them or giving them our phone number. There are many different ways in which we can help a newcomer. In doing so, we hope to be of service to them. But we do it primarily to strengthen and safeguard our own recovery.

The fifth measure which my sponsor suggested as a useful daily practice was to read some Fellowship literature. A paragraph or two from one of the basic texts is sufficient. Those who wish to range more widely around the many publications of the anonymous fellowships are encouraged to do so.

*Sixthly, said my sponsor, we should review our day before we go to bed. This is a good opportunity to practise Step Ten. We consider how our day has been spent: the good and useful things and the things which could be improved. More detailed suggestions are to be found in the **Actions** section of Chapter 15.*

Finally, before we close our eyes to sleep, we breathe a Thank You to our Higher Power for another day in recovery successfully concluded and for the gifts which the day has brought.

The seven suggestions above are nothing more than that — suggestions. As time goes by, most people modify them to suit their own individual circumstances. I no longer go to as many Meetings as I used to —or as I would like to. Nor do I phone my sponsor every single day.

These seven suggestions represent for me, not a legalistic or ritualistic formula, but an aspiration - an expression of the spirit of recovery. They are to be found in a more succinct format in Appendix II of this book. They are a simple way of practising the principles of the Twelve Step programme of recovery in our daily lives. The Twelve Step programme is a means of keeping our insanity at bay. It is a means of growing and of becoming whole. It is a path by which we may all come to understand, at least occasionally, what it means to be happy, joyous and free.

APPENDIX I – The Twelve Steps

(Adapted, with permission, from the 'Big Book' of Alcoholics Anonymous)

1. We admitted that we were powerless over our condition and that our lives had become unmanageable.

2. We came to believe that a power greater than ourselves could restore us to sanity.

3. We made a decision to turn our will and our lives over to the care of God as we understood Him.

4. We made a searching and fearless moral inventory of ourselves.

5. We admitted to God, to ourselves, and to another human being the exact nature of our wrongs.

6. We were entirely ready to have God remove all these defects of character.

7. We humbly asked God to remove our shortcomings.

8. We made a list of all persons we had harmed and became willing to make amends to them all.

9. We made direct amends to such people wherever possible, except when to do so would injure them or others.

10. We continued to take personal inventory and when we were wrong promptly admitted it.

11. We sought through prayer and meditation to improve our conscious contact with God as we understood Him, praying only for knowledge of His will for us and the power to carry that out.

12. Having had a spiritual awakening as the result of these steps, we tried to carry this message to those still in active addiction, and to practice these principles in all our affairs.

APPENDIX II - SEVEN THINGS DAILY

1. **Prayer and meditation** (first thing in the morning).

   a) Give thanks for the gift of another day and ask your Higher Power to help you to stay clean and sober TODAY.

   b) 3rd Step Prayer.

   c) Read **Just for Today** card (AA). Try, during the course of the day, to do everything on it. Don't worry if you cannot do it all perfectly. We aim for progress, not perfection!

   d) **Gratitude List**. Things you are grateful for *today*. Add to it daily.

   e) Anger and resentments. 'Pray for the bastards'. They might be sick.

   f) Any other prayers or meditations of your own choice (e.g. 7th Step Prayer if you have reached this Step).

2. **Contact your Sponsor** – either by phone or in person. Even if you're not having any particular problems, make it a habit to 'check in' with your Sponsor every day. Once you have progressed beyond Step Seven, this becomes less necessary.

3. **Get to a Meeting** – if at all possible, regardless of difficulties. Any meeting (in **any** of the Anonymous Fellowships) is better than no meeting at all. When you have progressed beyond Step Seven, *daily* meetings become less necessary.

4. **Help a newcomer.** A newcomer is anyone who has been in recovery for less time than you have – even if it's only a matter of days or hours! Helping them can just be giving them a cup of tea.

5. **Read some Fellowship literature**. It may be just a paragraph or two from the NA Basic Text, the AA Big Book, Twelve Steps and Twelve Traditions etc. It may be more.

6. **Review the day** before you go to bed. Do your Step 10. Try to see where you could have done things better, where faults must be admitted, where amends should be made.

7. **Say 'thank you'** to your Higher Power, before you go to sleep, for another day clean and sober.

APPENDIX III – ON RELAPSE

I shall not speak here of 'relapse prevention'. *One* of the many benefits of practising the Twelve Steps is that they prevent us from relapsing. But that is not what recovery is mainly about. Above all, it is about a more satisfying life.

When anyone who is in recovery from addictive disease 'picks up' a mood-altering drug or process, he or she is often said to have 'lapsed' or 'relapsed'. It is a false distinction. In order to 'lapse', we must first be in a state of relapse. Getting a liquid or substance inside us (or performing the actions of our addictive process) – these, in themselves, do **not** constitute a relapse. *They are simply a sign that we are already in a state of relapse.* They are the final stages of a long process.

As long as we continue, in each new day, to do the things that are necessary to maintain and develop our recovery, we are in a state of remission from our disease. If we neglect to do these things, we become sick again – just like the diabetic who neglects to take his insulin.

If somebody who has been in recovery from addictive disease picks up a mood-altering substance, liquid or process, it can mean many different things. But one of the things it *invariably* means is that this person is not working his or her Step One. Maybe they never really got to grips with Step One. Maybe they have temporarily lost sight of it. For whatever reason, it's not there when they need it. Let's remind ourselves of what Step One actually says:

Step One

We admitted that we were powerless over our condition (alcoholism, addiction etc.) and that our lives had become unmanageable.

If we are permanently and sufficiently conscious of our powerlessness over our addiction, we shall not want to step into the ring with it. Every time we 'pick up' we are stepping into the ring with our addictive disease. Our addictive disease is bigger and meaner and uglier and more powerful than we are. Every time we step into the boxing-ring with our addictive disease, it smashes us to pieces. We cannot afford to forget this. Most of us have done this often enough to know that it is true. We end up seriously battered and our lives become even more unmanageable. But sometimes we choose to forget it.

Before we 'pick up', we often begin to justify it to ourselves in some way. The 'stinking thinking' begins. 'Maybe I'm not really an addict, after all'. 'My only problem is heroin / cocaine / benzos – **not** alcohol / cannabis / speed'. 'I'll be able to get away with it'. 'I'll just do it for tonight. Nobody will know'.

If we were to mention any of these ideas to our fellows in recovery, they would soon show us how unrealistic they are. So we *don't* discuss them with our fellows in recovery. We begin to isolate ourselves. We start to 'put up the shutters'. We close up. Often we become secretive and devious again. Sometimes we collude in secret plans with others who are sick. These are frequently some of the first signs that we are falling into a state of relapse.

From this point on, the 'stinking thinking' continues – usually accompanied by the reappearance of old behaviour-patterns. Perhaps we lie in bed all day, instead of actively nourishing our recovery. We start missing out calls to our sponsor or we stop going to Meetings. We may begin to neglect our personal appearance or our domestic surroundings. Perhaps we distract ourselves from the personal changes on which we need to work by thinking obsessively about a 'relationship'. As long as we are obsessed with someone else, we do not have to look at ourselves.

Other addictive thoughts or behaviours may arise: compulsive overeating, undereating (anorexia), bulimia, gambling, compulsive sexual behaviours, compulsive risk-taking etc. All of these may be signs that we are already in 'relapse mode'. Addictive disease knows many different ways of reentering our lives. It is capable of creeping up on us surreptitiously.

If you have been unfortunate enough to succumb, in an unguarded moment, to the wiles of your disease, if you have 'picked up' or fallen into a state of relapse, it need not be a complete catastrophe. I personally needed every single relapse I suffered (and they were many) to get to a point where I began to understand the formidable power of my disease and began to become 'teachable'.

If necessary, return to the *Actions* section of Chapter 2 of this book (which deals with detoxification) – and then start again from where you left off. Begin to do the **Seven Things Daily** (Appendix II) again.

You can start your day at any time. It does not have to be the next morning. You can start your day right now. Once you have maintained abstinence for one day (24 hours), you are back on the road of recovery. You may find the attached worksheet helpful.

RECENT LAPSE OR RELAPSE – STEP ONE WORKSHEET

If I am honest with myself, do I notice that I engaged in any of the following behaviours or thought-processes, prior to using alcohol, other drugs or addictive processes? (In each case, give two or more specific examples):

1. *Isolating myself from other people in recovery?*

    a) physically   *(examples)*
    b) emotionally   *(examples)*
    c) not talking about urges/cravings   *(examples)*

2. *Becoming secretive or devious?*

    a) in my own thoughts and behaviours   *(examples)*
    b) in secret plans and activities with others   *(examples)*

3. *Have I been trying to 'fix myself' with an exclusive or codependent relationship?*   *(examples)*

4. *How have I tried to justify using drugs, alcohol or other addictive processes to myself?*   *(examples)*

5. *Have I fallen into 'old behaviour' patterns in respect of:*

    a) my personal care and appearance?   *(examples)*
    b) the care of my surroundings?   *(examples)*
    c) personal habits – sleep, eating, washing etc.? *(examples)*
    d) avoiding my family, social, community or economic responsibilities?
    (examples)

If we answer these questions honestly, we begin to get a sense of the power of our addictive disease – and of our own relative powerlessness in the face of it.

6. *Looking at each of the specific examples which you have noted above, suggest some ways in which you could have handled these situations differently. Decide how you will cope with them when similar circumstances arise in future.*

APPENDIX IV – On Legislation against Drugs

The AA 'Big Book', to which I have referred extensively, is, of course, a product of the early part of the twentieth century. To our modern sensibilities, the idiom in which it is written seems quaint and outmoded. Our knowledge, in some fields, has advanced since the time when it was written and we no longer share all of its cultural assumptions. Even in the field of recovery, we have had to revise some of the ideas of the early pioneers. They, indeed, predicted that this would happen. We know now, for instance, that *alcohol* is neither cunning, baffling nor powerful – as the 'Big Book' suggests. It's just a fairly toxic liquid. It is alcohol*ism* which is cunning, baffling and powerful. And alcoholism is just a form of addictive disease. And addictive disease is a manifestation of neurotransmission disease.

It is for this reason that legislation banning alcohol and other drugs is, at best, ineffective. At worst, it produces the very results which it seeks to counteract. It creates a populous criminal caste and a pervasive criminal culture. This, indeed, is what we saw during the American experiment with Prohibition of alcohol – and this is what we see today in respect of the other illegal drugs. Legislating in this way against drugs is like trying to eradicate measles by legislating against spots. The drugs, like the spots, are merely a symptom of the underlying disease. If assailed by the Law, the people with the spots will just go underground – and the worst consequences of the disease will continue to spread.

Naturally, access to potentially harmful substances needs to be controlled – particularly where minors are concerned. To some extent, the toxic drugs alcohol and tobacco are already controlled in this way.

However, as long as the extremely profitable supply of drugs is in the hands of the criminal fraternities, drug-crime and all of its attendant miseries will continue to flourish. On the other hand, the great advantage of the qualified legalisation of drugs is that it would place control of the supply of such drugs in the hands of the civil power. It would make it possible to have state-licensed pharmacies selling limited quantities of good quality (and quality-controlled) merchandise to people who can prove that they are legally adults and to regulate the supply and demand by means of taxation.

Details and quantities of all purchases and the identities of purchasers could thus be recorded, just as happens, at present, with the Poisons Register. Those who have severe addictions could be identified and, where appropriate, offered treatment. The prices of the various drugs (which would be designed to undercut any surviving 'black market') could be controlled by duties - and revenues thus raised could be usefully deployed to finance treatment centres.

Because, in the minds of the public, the erroneous assumptions and rhetoric of the so-called 'war on drugs' are now deeply embedded, it is unlikely that any government will have the courage to challenge the very ideas which successive governments have sought to inculcate.

A few experiments with decriminalisation have already been tried in some countries. The results, however, have been rather disappointing. This is because the mere **decriminalisation** of possession of small quantities of certain drugs for personal use will not serve the purpose. It leaves the *supply* of drugs in the hands of the criminals. Only qualified **legalisation** and effective control of the supply can produce the desired effects. Politicians, who, wittingly or unwittingly, have fostered public ignorance of the real issues, are now unlikely to risk the displeasure of an electorate conditioned to expect policies which are 'tough on drugs'. Governments, therefore, may be expected to continue tinkering with the legislation against spots.

It remains true, nevertheless, that you can no more remove the evils arising from addictive disease by legislating against drugs than you can cure headaches by legislating against aspirin.

APPENDIX V

GLOSSARY OF ADDICTION AND RECOVERY TERMS

AA: See 'Fellowship'.

abstinence: to abstain from using the substances or processes of addiction. Mere abstinence is not the same as recovery *(q.v.)*. However, abstinence is necessary before recovery can begin *(cf. 'detox')*.

addictive disease: the condition which underlies many addictive-compulsive behaviours. It appears to be a disease involving both mood and perception and is probably related to inherited deficiencies in the neuro-transmission systems. It manifests itself primarily in a dysfunction of mood, feeling and emotion. The individual behaviours *(addictive disorders q.v.)* to which addictive disease gives rise (drug-taking, drinking, starving etc.) may be seen as attempts to 'medicate' this underlying condition.

addictive disorder: one of the many different ways in which addictive disease *(q.v. above)* may manifest itself – drug using, alcohol misuse, compulsive overeating, anorexia, bulimia, compulsive gambling, compulsive sexual behaviours, compulsive risk-taking, etc., etc. Each of the addictive disorders may be seen both as a symptom of the underlying addictive disease and as an attempt to medicate this condition. The behaviours associated with addictive disorders share three principal characteristics. They are excessive, they are mood-altering and they give rise to increasingly negative consequences in the lives of sufferers and of other people who come into contact with them.

anonymous fellowships: loosely organised fellowships of men and women who wish to recover from the different manifestations of addictive disease. The first was Alcoholics Anonymous. This was followed by Narcotics Anonymous and, more recently, by a range of increasingly specialised fellowships (Overeaters Anonymous, Cocaine Anonymous, Sex and Love Addicts Anonymous etc.). They are all underpinned by the Twelve Step programme of recovery (q.v.) and by the principle of anonymity.

anorexia: abbreviated form of the medical term *anorexia nervosa*, denoting a condition characterised by compulsive starving or under-eating. Sufferers often exhibit an irrational fear of nourishment and may perceive themselves as 'fat' – no matter how emaciated they appear to others. Anorexia is often associated with adolescent girls but may, in fact, affect people of both genders and of any age.

Big Book: The AA 'Big Book' is actually entitled *Alcoholics Anonymous*. It was first published in 1939 and the fellowship of AA took its name from the book.

bulimia: abbreviated form of the medical term *bulimia nervosa*, denoting a condition characterised by compulsive gorging ('bingeing' on food) usually followed by self-induced vomiting. Bulimia, though most common among young women, may affect people of both genders and of any age.

chair: see 'share'

clean-time: term used, especially in NA, to denote the length of time (in days, months or years) that an individual has remained abstinent from drugs and in recovery. In NA, different coloured key rings are awarded to people for varying amounts of 'clean-time'.

cluck: unpleasant sensations accompanying withdrawal from drugs. Used as verb or noun. *cf* cold turkey, rattle etc.

cold turkey: withdrawal from drugs, usually implying abrupt cessation without substitute drugs.

compulsive: compulsive behaviours are behaviours which are characterised by overwhelming and almost irresistible compulsion (e.g. compulsive overeating). All addictions are compulsive behaviours.

dealer: one who supplies illegal drugs for money or other types of payment.

denial: refusal or inability to acknowledge the increasingly damaging consequences of addiction. Denying to oneself or to others that there is a problem.

detox: short for 'detoxification'. In the context of addictions and of their treatment it denotes the process by which an individual is separated from his or her substance or process of addiction. Used to be called 'drying out' in relation to alcohol misuse. May also be used as a verb. 'She's detoxing', 'He's being detoxed'. *cf* rattle, cold turkey etc.

disease model (of addiction): an understanding of addiction which sees it as an identifiable disease, possibly genetically transmitted, with a specified set of signs and symptoms and a definable progression.

Fellowship: one of the Anonymous Fellowships of people in recovery from addictive disorders (Alcoholics Anonymous, Narcotics Anonymous, Overeaters Anonymous, Gamblers Anonymous, Sex and Love Addicts Anonymous, etc.) e.g. 'Is he in the Fellowship?' May also be used as an adjective e.g. 'Fellowship literature' (see p.10).

Higher Power: any power defined by the individual as being greater than himself or herself and capable of assisting recovery.

lapse: see 'relapse'.

lifestory: a therapeutic exercise, favoured in many treatment centres, in which the patient delivers an account of his or her life to a group of fellow recovering peers.

Minnesota Method, Minnesota Model: method of treatment developed in Minnesota for the treatment of addictive disorders. It deploys group-therapy to mediate an intensive introduction to the Twelve Step programme of recovery.

NA: see 'Fellowship'.

rattle: name applied to the sensations experienced during the final stages of drug withdrawal or detoxification. Disagreeable sensations caused by the absence of drugs in an individual whose metabolism has become accustomed to high blood levels of a particular chemical.

recovery: term denoting the process by which people recover from active addiction. Recovery is best promoted by abstinence from the substance or process of addiction and by far-reaching personal change.

rehab: the process of rehabilitation from active addiction (e.g. 'she's in rehab') or the place where this process occurs (e.g. 'he's in a rehab').

relapse: *to* relapse is to return to a condition of addiction after a period in recovery. *A* relapse is the state thus resumed. It is not necessary to use drink or drugs to be in a state of relapse. The use of these substances (or of other addictive processes) is simply a sign that the individual is already in a state of relapse. The word 'lapse' is sometimes used to denote a brief 'using' episode. It is a false distinction. In order to 'lapse', we must first be in a state of relapse.

share: to speak about personal experience of addiction and recovery, especially in a Meeting of one of the Anonymous Fellowships. May also be used as a noun *(e.g. to do or give a share)*. The word 'chair' may also be used to refer to a formal share.

sober, sobriety: in AA, the condition of being abstinent from alcohol and practising the programme of recovery. AAs often distinguish between being merely 'dry' (reluctantly abstinent) and being 'sober' (in recovery).

sponsee: *see 'sponsor'*

sponsor: an experienced member of one of the anonymous fellowships who is able to help less experienced members (sponsees) to practise the programme of recovery. This help is given free because the sponsor's own recovery is strengthened by helping others. A sponsor is usually of the same gender as the sponsee.

treatment: the process of being treated for addictive disorders in a 'Treatment Centre' or 'rehab' (q.v.), usually residential. e.g. 'She's in treatment'.

trigger situation: believed by some to be a situation in which an addict is most likely to 'use'. High-risk situation.

Twelve Steps: the programme of recovery first elaborated by the earliest members of Alcoholics Anonymous and later adopted by other anonymous fellowships. The Twelve Steps also form the basis of the 'Minnesota' method of treatment (q.v.).

using, to use: the addictive use of any substance, liquid or process.

READER NOTES

READER NOTES

Additional copies of this book may be obtained from your local bookseller or by post from:

The Sow's Ear Press
School House, Alby Hill
Aldborough, Norwich
Norfolk NR11 7PH
UK

Cheques should be made payable to **The Sow's Ear Press**
(£9.99 per copy + £1.33 shipping for up to 4 copies). For discounts on larger orders please phone 01263 768554.

No Big Deal is also available from www.nobigdeal.org.uk, from www.sowsearpress.co.uk or from www.amazon.co.uk